THE LIBRARY
ST. MARY'S COLLEGE OF MARYLAND
ST. MARY'S CITY, MARYLAND 20686

THE CRAFT OF NON-FICTION

THE CRAFT OF NON-FICTION

william c. knott
state university of new york at potsdam

reston publishing company, inc.
a prentice-hall company
reston, virginia 22090

Library of Congress Cataloging in Publication Data

Knott, Bill, 1927–
　　The craft of non-fiction.

　　1.　Authorship.　I.　Title.
PN145.K64　　　　808'.02　　74-6465
ISBN 0-87909-161-4
ISBN 0-87909-160-6 (pbk.)

© 1974 by
Reston Publishing Company, Inc.
A Prentice-Hall Company
P.O. Box 547
Reston, Virginia 22090

All rights reserved. No part of this book
may be reproduced in any way, or by any
means, without permission in writing from
the publisher.

10 9 8 7 6 5 4 3 2 1

Printed in the United States of America

contents

PREFACE   ix

PART ONE: THE WORLD OF NON-FICTION   1

CHAPTER ONE:
THIS VERY EXCITING PROFESSION   3

The prospects were never better. What you as a beginning writer can expect.

CHAPTER TWO: THE NATURE OF THE BEAST   7

The limits of non-fiction. The need non-fiction satisfies.

CHAPTER THREE:
CAN YOU WRITE NON-FICTION?   13

Are you curious? Are you serious?

PART TWO: NUTS AND BOLTS 17

CHAPTER FOUR:
LOOK AT ALL THOSE MAGAZINES 19

Sources for the news feature. Personalities. Narratives. Self-help. How-to-do-it.

CHAPTER FIVE:
BUT WHAT DOES IT ALL MEAN? 31

Why theme is necessary. How to make use of your theme. Formulating your theme. No propaganda please.

CHAPTER SIX:
WHO'S TALKING HERE, ANYWAY? 37

Which point-of-view to choose.

CHAPTER SEVEN:
PLEASE . . . YOU'RE PUTTING ME TO SLEEP 43

Flatness in your style. Variety in sentence structure. Circumlocution. Unintelligibility. Paragraphing.

CHAPTER EIGHT: GET THE FACTS 53

The library. The card catalogue. The special library. Public relations offices. The government. Professional organizations. Newspaper files. Chamber of commerce. Consular offices. The telephone. The interview. Transcribing the interview. Using copyrighted material. What about pictures?

PART THREE: THE ACT OF WRITING 71

CHAPTER NINE:
I'D LIKE TO WRITE ABOUT THAT 73

Your hobbies. Don't bite off more than you can chew. Is it a researchable topic? How much time and money can you afford to invest on speculation?

CHAPTER TEN: DEAR EDITOR   79

Finding the target.   Preliminary research.   The query letter.   After sending the query.

CHAPTER ELEVEN:
MY AUNT WAS MARRIED TO A GORILLA   85

The direct address hook.   Hooking the reader with a question.   The startling fact as hook.   The narrative hook.   The summary hook.   Length of the hook.   Titles.

CHAPTER TWELVE:
PUTTING IT ALL TOGETHER   95

The outline: order out of chaos.   Writing the first draft.   The need for revision.   How to rewrite.   A checklist.   Fitting in the corrections.   The final draft.   Should you hire a typist?

CHAPTER THIRTEEN:
GETTING – AND STAYING – PUBLISHED   105

Some typing hints.   Submitting the manuscript.   Should your article be copyrighted before you submit it?   Keeping a record.   The return of the prodigal.   Do you need an agent?   What do you do while waiting to hear?   You and the market.   How much money can you expect?   Specializing.

CHAPTER FOURTEEN:
NOW THAT YOU ARE A WRITER   117

Do you need more research?   The daily schedule.   Does it get any easier?

INDEX   121

preface

To the young writer who might chafe at the sometimes pedantic tone of this text, I counsel patience. When the writer reaches maturity, he or she will have an opportunity to pronounce his or her own dogma. But until that time the writer might find it useful to accept this text for what it is: simply one possible way to proceed through the thicket of conflicting advice to the practice of a demanding yet fascinating profession.

At one time or another all rules of rhetoric are broken, usually for good and judicious reasons. Undoubtedly many imperatives enunciated herein will be discarded or supplanted as well. But experience alone will give the writer the knowledge he or she will need to make these decisions. Until then this text is simply a demonstration of those few but effective principles or forms found useful by many of today's writers. It is nothing more, nothing less; and all it can hope to do is help the young writer along the path he or she must ultimately travel alone.

William C. Knott

THE CRAFT OF NON-FICTION

part one

THE WORLD OF NON-FICTION

What does the profession of free-lance writer of non-fiction hold for you? Is it really your cup of tea? Was your high school English teacher correct when he or she said that you were a born writer? Perhaps this first part will not really answer **all** of these questions; but it may answer a few and put you on the track to answering the rest for yourself.

chapter one

This Very Exciting Profession

First the good news. When we consider the prospects for the writer of non-fiction today, it is difficult not to be optimistic. This world, more often than not, resembles a circus on fire, with a vast audience clamoring for all the grisly details— and a wealth of publications anxious to sate that appetite. For the writer of non-fiction willing to work, that's good news indeed.

Not so long ago it was the writer of fiction the magazine and book publishers courted. In response to the mood and demand of the times, they published three times as much fiction as non-fiction. Today that ratio is reversed. The non-fiction boom is on, for both books and magazine articles. The writer of non-fiction—if he or she can write—is someone very much in demand these days.

Why is this? Well, if this world is in trouble, the diagnosis might well be a cholesterol of poorly digested fact clogging the arteries leading to the brain. What, after all, are the facts concerning the safety of our new drugs, new power reactors, the state of our oceans, our lungs, the level of DDT in our livers; what or who really started the last three wars? What's normal? Who's normal? Define a criminal. Has democracy ever worked for long?

We look to the writer of non-fiction to give us a decent start in answering some of those questions.

The Prospects Were Never Better

The magazines proliferating now, and those that have survived the past twenty years, are devoted almost entirely to non-fiction. The family-oriented, general magazine has given way to the magazine that caters to the specialist. We have mass circulation magazines dealing with sex, psychology, science, human behavior, family health, organic gardening, babies, motorcycles, stereophonic music, automobiles, stock car racing, consumers, snowmobiles, flying, and boating. And though we still have that famous digest for readers, we now have a digest for intellectuals as well.

Every month or so in today's non-fiction market new magazines are popping to the surface. *Playboy* recently launched a new magazine called *Oui*, aimed at a younger audience than *Playboy*'s. At the same time another new magazine, *Gallery*, set up its offices across the street from the Playboy Building in Chicago and announced it was interested in timely articles for a young, avant-garde audience and would pay a flat rate of $750 for each manuscript.... A new book publisher, Arthur Fields Books, Inc., announced it was looking for commercial non-fiction, including subject novels, first-person accounts, journalism of substance.... Thetis Powers of *Sexology* magazine, in response to a query, said she would like to see articles on all aspects of sexuality: medical, sociological, personal—including first-person reports....

The following month *McCalls'* editors announced they were looking for newsworthy items concerning all aspects of women's lives. . . . a new magazine, *Dogs*, "The Magazine For Everyone Who Enjoys Them," is now looking for articles from anyone who can write informatively and entertainingly about dogs. ... A brand new magazine, *Diversion*, will soon be hitting the stands, and the editors say that they will be looking for material for doctors that is consumer oriented. This is a magazine designed, in short, to divert those in the medical profession. ... A new magazine, *On the Mall*, finds itself in the market for general interest articles, as well as fashions, food, beauty, films, books, and music features. New writers are welcome.

This was but a sampling of the activity for two months prior to the publication of this text. By the time you read this, of course, still more markets will have appeared. All of which means that there is a burgeoning, voracious market out there waiting for your articles.

What You as a Beginning Writer Can Expect

Since many of the finest, most imaginative writers alive today are now writing non-fiction, you can expect some very stiff competition. Most likely, as a beginner, you will have to get your feet wet gradually in less prestigious publications before you will be able to sell to the better paying ones. But don't be impatient. Instant success is rarely possible in free-lancing, for the writer is only as good as the sources he or she is able to develop over the years. Most of the overnight successes in this field have spent ten years or more learning their craft. But this is a field where as a beginning writer you can earn while you learn.

Questions For Study and Discussion

1. When you have a few moments to relax with a magazine or book, which do you prefer, fiction or non-fiction?
2. When books or articles are discussed in your circle of friends, isn't the discussion about the facts — bothersome or otherwise — that are gleaned from them? Have you noticed how infrequently the contents of fictional works are discussed on the TV talk shows? How often it is the authors of non-fiction who are interviewed?

chapter two
The Nature of the Beast

The distinction between writing fiction and non-fiction is one that too many students fail to make. When reflecting on their decision to make a career as a writer of non-fiction, many usually confess to the deep solace they derived from venting their private gripes on paper; or how they loved to keep diaries whenever they went anywhere special; or how poetic their teachers thought their writing was. Perhaps so. But despite apparent similarities, non-fiction is not fiction; it is a different beast entirely, and that difference is the burden of this chapter.

What is needed in non-fiction is not really a gift for the poetic flight of fancy or an urge to unburden oneself of half-baked, but very sincere notions on how the world should be run. What is needed are facts—mind-boggling, verifiable facts that settle arguments and arouse to action:

In April of this year, Alfred Mendel, a psychiatrically certified "sane and normal" individual, confessed to nine killings and led police to nine mutilated, decomposing bodies, scattered in shallow graves over the New Mexican countryside. Among the bodies was that of his own mother. She had been decapitated....

In 1941 William L. Armstrong was a business failure in St. Paul. Today, a vital and energetic eighty-two, he is preparing to rule the world from his and God's headquarters in Carmel, California.

In 1970, Centralia had the third highest rate of leukemia in the state of Kansas . . . and the fourth highest rate of immature births....

Of the total coating volume, the oxide particles occupy only about 30 to 40 percent. If, in an effort to achieve a greater signal output, more oxide were to be put on the recording tape, a weaker cohesion of the coating would result. This in turn would seriously hamper the flexibility of the tape in handling frequencies higher than....

The amount of digging required to unearth such "facts" may well cause many a neophyte to pause. And it should. But the facts are there. The hours spent researching those facts always pay off, both in lending substance to an article and—in many cases—providing still further material for other articles.

Here's an example:

A young writer became interested in doing a story on a local marriage counselor who seemed to have phenomenal success. He interviewed her and found her methods prosaic enough, but became interested in her case histories. He did considerable research on the whole matter of marriage counseling and this, together with his interview with the counselor, gave him three feature articles: one on the counselor herself, another on which women make the best wives, and a third on the factors that made for successful reconciliations. His expertise with this kind of article eventually led him, years later, to write a book on marriage counseling.

Flights of fancy would have been useless to this writer, likewise a penchant for the poetic. What helped him and what can help any other beginning writer is the knowledge that without facts nothing much can happen; but that with them much good writing can be accomplished.

The Limits of Non-fiction

Since non-fiction is not fiction, it is essential that at no time do you allow the lack of appropriate facts to cajole you into inventing them. Invention is not forbidden in writing non-fiction. A great deal of creative thinking goes into the writing of any article, but it is of a different variety from that which goes into the writing of fiction.

One writer wrote a "true" account of his fishing exploits off an imaginary island in the Gulf of Mexico, and had it published as fact by one of the sports magazines. He had a rude awakening when several readers set out for his fictitious isle and then reported their findings back to the editor. The writer had one devil of a time keeping afloat in the writing business after that gaffe, since editors like to swap information on their various contributors.

Don't make this kind of mistake. Fact is fact and fiction is fiction. Don't get them mixed up, even if the lack of appropriate source material means you have to abandon what you felt was an appealing subject.

The Need Non-fiction Satisfies

Interestingly enough, non-fiction is very much like fiction in that is satisfies almost the same needs. For some people, non-fiction seems to be a cut above fiction. They reason this way: fiction attempts to save our sanity with fairy tales that mask the truth, but non-fiction attempts that same cure with facts—that is, with the truth. Be that as it may, non-fiction and fiction are similar in the needs they satisfy; and an examination of those needs will help clarify this point.

People are interested in people. Of course facts are important, and we're not going to forget that. But a string of unadorned facts has little interest until it is shown how these facts affect specific individuals. The human equation is vital if there is to be much interest in what you write. Reference librarians will tell you all you need to know about an industry or an organization, but until you relate this to real personalities, you won't have much of an article. This is because people find it easier to visualize human situations than vague abstractions. An article that describes in general terms the danger that an atomic power plant could represent to a major city may have difficulty convincing the reader and may end up sounding more than a little shrill. On the other hand, an article about a little girl dying in a hospital because she picked up a radioactive isotope while playing in an abandoned lot alongside that hospital is another thing entirely.

An article concerning a scandal of widespread cheating in a major military school can only be brought into focus by zeroing in on the two cadets who, because of their involvement, are forced to leave the academy. The dimensions of the problem at that academy—the erosion of values it represents, the tragedies such lapses produce—are vast and complex. A discussion of the two individuals immediately concerned, however, makes the problem personal and clear-cut. And this the reader wants to be let in on; this the reader wants to feel. Whether it is fiction or non-fiction, this is why the reader reads. The spectacle of another human being in some dire fix has the greatest drawing power of any single event. Morbid or not, it's there. In all of us.

In fiction, writers take an appealing character striving against great odds to attain a worthwhile goal and follow him or her through to the accomplishment of that goal. Though much non-fiction tells this same story, it tells it not as fiction, but as the unvarnished truth. As in fiction, the good non-fiction writer pits the hero or heroine—the subject of the article—against nature, or against man, or society, or even him- or herself, not forgetting to mix in the indispensable elements of all good drama: economics, personalities, ethics, and love.

Consider the individual astronauts as they readied themselves for their trip to the moon; consider the drama, the conflict engendered when a once-great football coach comes out of retirement to prove himself once again in professional football; consider Amelia Earhart's story; the rise of Hitler; the curious and tragic detours on the way to any political career in this country. To relate these triumphs and sorrows factually, and yet dramatically, is to enable the reader to satisfy a need for the dramatic that is well-nigh unquenchable.

The other need filled by non-fiction is significance. True, human interest, oddity, or drama may by themselves be enough to intrigue the reader, but unless all of this human interest and drama can somehow be related to the person reading the article or book, the reader's response is most likely a casual, "Well, that's interesting," or a not so casual, "So what?"

The reader wants to know how he or she is affected by it all. So the stock market is falling; what's the significance of this fact to him? Should he buy or sell? The job market is glutted with

Ph.D's. Should she quit college? In short, though non-fiction satisfies the reader's need to know and his or her desire for excitement and diversion, it has little meaning for the reader unless it is woven around a central core of significance—if not for the reader personally, then for many of his or her contemporaries.

Questions for Study and Discussion

1. What famous works of non-fiction can you recall that told the story of one solitary individual's battle against fate?
2. Why do you suppose one of the leading sellers today is *The Guinness Book of World Records?*
3. Discuss the number of non-fiction books that are constructed around a famous or interesting personality or event. What is their appeal?
4. Bring in any women's or men's magazine and discuss the articles in terms of their significance and dramatic impact for the average reader.

chapter three

Can You Write Non-fiction?

Make no mistake about it. This factor of always being tied to the actual, to what you can document, can be a most irritating condition of your employment. The desire to reach back into your imagination and wing it may be too much for you. But if you are one of those who reads fiction only when nothing else offers itself, then perhaps the writing of non-fiction is for you.

But let's read on to make sure.

Some writers of non-fiction have confessed that *writing* non-fiction is almost the easiest part of the task. This is understandable, for before you can begin to write, you must first have all the facts. Without adequate research, little of any real importance can happen.

Research is always necessary in any form of writing, of course, but in non-fiction fact is absolutely essential. The positive side to this is that, by the time you do sit down to write, your article or your book should practically pour out of you, almost writing itself as the hours of research, interviewing, and background reading come to the fore. But remember: I said *almost*. The craft is still needed to shape that flow.

Researching, interviewing, and chasing down leads are difficult and time-consuming, a far cry perhaps from the contemplative den where you might have expected to hole up while you pursued your writing career. In short, you must be a working scholar, as familiar with libraries as with people, able to pick up and move out on a moment's notice, and not at all shy about interviewing people of all kinds and sizes.

One writer, in order to gain the confidence of a Harlem pusher for his book on the Harlem scene, had to go everywhere with the pusher, since the fellow refused to use phones. Finally, in order to gain the pusher's trust, he had to take cocaine. Another writer, preparing an article on prostitution, found herself turning tricks herself, using one of the prostitute's John Books to drum up customers. Another writer had to submit to the ministrations of one of New York City's Dr. Feelgoods in order to expose these doctors' illegal use of amphetamines, which they shoot into the ample buttocks and veins of those patients rich enough to afford such treatments. These, of course, are somewhat extreme examples; but in today's journalism where the motto is obviously: "Go out and get the facts, first hand!" this sort of thing is not unknown.

Less exciting, perhaps, but just as necessary is a willingness to spend hours in libraries digging for facts. Sometimes when it seems that there are no facts for you to discover, you must simply continue to dig and dig and dig.

Are You Curious?

Not too long ago *Writer's Digest* devoted an entire issue to the theme of curiosity, for this trait, its editors felt, was the one single ingredient every writer had in common. And, of course, the editors were right. You can always pick out the writer in a group. He's curious, sincerely curious. He listens. He asks questions, and astounds the people he questions by listening intently to their answers.

Writers read voraciously and widely. They may not be experts in the scholarly sense, but they know a great deal about a wide range of subjects. Everything is regarded as grist for their mill. The non-writer reads, but what he or she reads simply solidifies or deepens interests already held. But the writer—and the would-be writer—is constantly delving in his or her reading into every imaginable field.

Are You Serious?

Do you write only when you are in the mood? Do you have an excellent idea for an article or book that you plan to tackle as soon as you get that two-week vacation in the mountains you've been hoping for? As soon as a friend of yours gets the name of a good agent in New York, are you going to write this agent and inquire about copyrighting an article you have in mind? Have you been seriously thinking about writing a book about your experiences in the Second World War? If your answer to any of these questions is yes, you are not serious enough about a writing career.

Waiting for inspiration to spur you to the desk is like waiting for Godot, and not nearly as instructive. Of course, sometimes you actually will write under the fire of inspiration—but not because you waited for it, for writing does not come that easily. There are other primary functions of the human being that come much easier than wringing the brain out over a typewriter. The best way to face this toil is to transform it into a *habit*; this is what the professional writer does.

You see, as a writer your problem is that you have no clock to punch. There is no boss glowering over your shoulder, no teacher pleading for the assignment. When you really become established as a professional, you will have an editor waiting, usually with a deadline to meet. But not always. Until that time, you must be the one to set deadlines and to ride herd on your progress or lack of it.

The question thus becomes: Can you do this as well, and for as long as it might take to establish yourself?

In summary, you can write non-fiction if you are ready to live with the realities of the profession. It takes hard work to put it all together. This is not to say that the writing profession does not offer tangible rewards, both personal and financial; indeed, most writers would want no other occupation.

Yet unless you share with them their skill in research, their desire to know just about everything under the sun—and can tie all this together with a willingness to spend long hours in front of a typewriter, you might better consider seriously your alternatives to a writing career.

On the other hand, if all this simply recharges your desire to write non-fiction, if little said in this chapter discourages you, then read on.

Questions for Study and Discussion

1. How much writing have you done already? When did you first start writing? Discuss critically previous writing—such as school newspaper, stringer for local weekly or daily, and so on.
2. How familiar are you with libraries? When you read, is it primarily for information or entertainment? Whichever it is, examine closely your motives for this preference.

Suggestions for Writing

1. Your library should have back copies of both *Writer's Digest* and *The Writer*. Search through these magazines for accounts given by various free-lance writers of how they made it as selling professionals. Select one such writer and write an account of what he or she went through. Don't overlook the letters column in both magazines.
2. Write a short biography of yourself up to this point, covering primarily your development as a writer.
3. Interview any local free-lance writer. (Check the editorial staff of your local newspaper first for likely candidates.) Ask him or her to discuss with you the pitfalls and rewards of a career as a writer and write this interview up for distribution to class members. *Suggestion*: You might take a small cassette tape recorder along on the interview and transcribe it as a straight question-and-answer *Playboy* type interview.

part two
NUTS AND BOLTS

By now you must be anxious to get going. But hold on. There are some mechanical items that need to be tended to first—what I call the Nuts and Bolts of writing. During this portion of the text you will be laying the necessary groundwork for the preparation of your own articles.

chapter four

Look at All Those Magazines

When you first survey the market for non-fiction, you may see only a bewildering confusion of magazines and article types. Anxious to get in front of a typewriter and go to work, you will ask yourself what kind of article should you write, and for which magazine?

What follows is a brief survey of article types; depending on the subject matter exploited, the usual source of material for particular types; and, in most cases, the appropriate markets for these kinds of articles.

The *news feature* is often the easiest to master and is the type of article most beginning writers try first. This kind of article springs from current news and concerns, local, national, or international.

Any celebrity who returns to his or her home town after making it big, or a local person who becomes successful in his or her own backyard is material for the news feature, as long as the news peg for the article is some current event or award that brings the subject to the attention of many people.

Let's say that Jackson Jones returns to his home town after paddling alone across the Atlantic in a rubber life raft. Now, tanned and healthy, he is experiencing a royal welcome. After riding in an open convertible through town with the mayor and his proud parents, he gives a speech to an assembly of local high school students before addressing the Rotary that same night. Altmira, North Dakota is on the map.

Suppose you live in that town or within driving distance. This celebration offers material for a sheaf of articles that would be gobbled up by local and regional newspapers and magazines. A study of the town, with the emphasis on what the townspeople's feelings are concerning Mr. Jones, would make a fine article for a national Sunday supplement of local and regional newspapers.

An interview with the famous man himself could explore the motives that caused him to cross the Atlantic in this fashion and what his plans were for the future. Did the Pacific already beckon? Unless he had already contracted with a publisher for the exclusive rights to his story, *Argosy* or *True Magazine* might be more than interested in an as-told-to article on his experiences while crossing the Atlantic. And you would write it.

Of course I am exaggerating here to make my point. Much less spectacular things happen to local boys and girls who return to their home town. A congresswoman from a nearby district could suddenly find herself making headlines as the result of a probe of some scandal or other in Washington. At once there will be interest in the woman and in her background. A quick ride to her home town and interviews with old teachers and friends and acquaintances should give you excellent material for a background piece on the congresswoman.

Or perhaps a local man suddenly blossoms forth as the writer of a sexy historical novel. An interview with him could be sent to a writer's magazine; and if his success begins to swell, another story could be written on the reaction of the townspeople to the sudden emergence in their midst of this new talent. Have they read the book? Are they outraged at the frankly explicit sex? How has his wife managed to stand up under the glare of publicity?

On a somewhat more prosaic level, a local businesswoman

running an insurance agency may suddenly get an award for her agency's sales record. An interview with her, exploring how she managed to inspire her salespeople to this degree of effectiveness, could find a place in any trade magazine that caters to the insurance field—as well as to the local newspaper for a Sunday feature.

Sometimes your community itself becomes the center of a burgeoning news story, as when the citizens suddenly arouse themselves to stop the construction of a major elevated highway through a section of town. Committees are formed. Delegations are sent to the state house to badger the legislature. As the campaign grows in intensity, you will find the raw material for news features everywhere.

Imagine the human interest potential of a story based on the plight of an elderly couple who suddenly find they are about to lose the home in which they have spent a lifetime. Their children have all grown. They have nowhere else to go. This home was to have been their shelter and their comfort in their old age. Another article could explore the bitter feelings this situation arouses between those townspeople who want to sell out at a good price and those who don't. An article with the title "A Town at War with Itself" could be sent to *Grit* or *Parade* or any other of the Sunday supplements published nationally.

Sources for the News Feature

Every community contains authorities of one kind or another, and you should make a list of those individuals in the community who may be considered authorities in their fields. Nor should you forget that each successful businessperson—including the local beekeeper—is an authority on his or her business and therefore a source of news and information.

Acutely interested in this kind of article is the enormous trade journal market which specializes in publishing articles on how storekeepers, managers, and owners of businesses manage to keep afloat and prospering in our economy. At last count the number of these magazines had reached something over 2,500, with titles ranging from *Tire Review* and *Western Floors* to *Armed Forces Management*.

Still another source for the news feature article is the calendar of community events, usually put out by the local chamber of commerce. With this list in hand, you could note what conventions were scheduled, and what parades or celebrations. The opening of a new municipal swimming pool could be covered for the local newspaper and possibly for the Sunday supplement of a large regional newspaper nearby.

But most important of all, since the news feature is an article that takes a bit of news as its seed and goes on from there to elaborate and amplify it, the most obvious source for news features is the local newspaper itself. An account of a tractor-trailer pile up on a local high speed expressway, as a news item, would be confined to the accident itself. But as the writer of a news feature article that examines the accident thoroughly you might well point up the need for an additional lane at this increasingly crowded exit, citing recent accidents and near misses at this same spot. This article, in turn, might well find a place in the local newspaper's Sunday supplement.

A news item concerning a local crop duster forced to land his plane on a busy highway on a foggy morning could lead to an article about the hazards of crop dusting—from the lethal spray itself to the dangers inherent in any low-flying acrobatics.

In ways such as this, as an alert writer, you will find that the newspaper is a more than ample source for the news feature article.

Personalities

People—as emphasized earlier—like to read about other people: neighbors, famous writers, explorers, movie and TV stars.

Some editors differentiate between the personality sketch and the profile; the latter they define as a study that zeroes in on a person vis-a-vis his or her career; while the personality sketch, they feel, emphasizes the person's character, philosophy, and outlook on life. In short, the profile highlights what the person has done; the personality sketch, what the person is.

In practice, however, it is often difficult, if not unwise, to make this distinction, since what a person accomplishes depends to such a great extent on what kind of a person he or she is to begin with. For this reason, more and more editors and writers today are calling both types profiles, allowing the profile to focus on the subject's career or personality as the material itself directs.

Who are the best subjects for profiles? Start with any well-known or successful person living in your community, not forgetting to consider the local industrial leader or sportsman. If you live in Hollywood or New York, you will have no difficulty at all in finding subjects for a profile. But not all writers live in these two celebrity capitals.

Look around, therefore, for persons who are of interest simply because of their unusual characteristics or for their fresh way of looking at life. A butcher who publishes a book of poetry is bound to be of interest to readers. If you can find a local personality who combines success in his or her career with an exciting, spicy personality, you have a perfect subject for your profile.

On the other hand, Mr. Average Guy can also be interesting enough for an article *if he is typical*. His very normalcy can be a peg on which to hang an article. Think of the problems encountered by the average GI home from Southeast Asia trying to cope with this hectic American society after four years in Viet-Nam. Or take the fellow who shows what he's made of by overcoming a severe physical handicap.

At the moment there is a great deal of mileage being gained with the celebrity interview in which the person conducting the interview is labeled: INTERVIEWER, with his or her question quoted verbatim, and the celebrity's answer quoted just as directly. At the beginning of such articles, the author sometimes describes the scene where the interview takes place and gives a quick thumbnail sketch of the subject of the interview. In these interview-articles a great deal depends on just how tenacious and alert the interviewer is in following up the answers given by the celebrity and in digging deeply enough to reveal more than the surface of the subject.

As can be imagined, however, the people being interviewed must be newsworthy in their own right, or few will care to read what they have to say—and that includes editors. The problem for the beginner here, then, is that most famous or well-known people will not allow their time to be taken up by anyone who is obviously a neophyte or who does not represent a fairly well-known magazine. Of course, there are exceptions, and if you happen to find a big name who is willing to sit still for a session with you, you might very well find yourself with a salable article.

Almost all of the popular publications are looking for profiles, with the already mentioned trade journals as eager as the rest. Writers' magazines are looking for profiles or interview-articles on successful writers, coach's magazines are receptive to those done on successful coaches. Even profiles of youngsters who have achieved some special award or distinction will find a place in the pages of *The Young Catholic Messenger*, *Seventeen*, or *Boys Life*. Lodge and fraternal magazines are always interested in personality and success stories.

Narratives

As the heading suggests, the narrative article is one that is presented almost fictionally and, most surely, dramatically. This type can be broken up into three variants: the exciting single incident or episode, the adventure article, and finally the article that makes its point by collecting a series of typical incidents. The locale for these articles can be anywhere in the world and the time can be the past, the present, even the future if you're building carefully on fact.

The single electrifying incident is quite popular today, since it is usually short—and the emphasis in many of today's popular magazines is toward brevity. Specific examples of this variety would be the account of an individual's escape from a burning ocean liner or hotel fire; an individual's account of his rescue by helicopter after crashing in an isolated area; the story of an escape from an unfriendly shark; or the tale of a bar invaded by members of a motorcycle gang.

Finding subjects for this kind of article should be relatively easy. And it is with this sort of as-told-to article that the technique of the interview becomes of paramount importance, since it is only by speaking with and questioning those people who habitually find themselves in such predicaments that you can obtain the raw material for your article. The subjects to be interviewed in search of such material would be detectives, airplane pilots, hunters, explorers, civil engineers, and any others whose work brings them constantly into touch with those incidents and episodes calculated to arouse the adrenalin of the average reader.

Usually the interview begins with the question: "What was your most exciting experience?" And what you get for an answer is the framework on which you build your article.

An extension of the single episode article is the adventure article in which a long chain of exciting events are linked to make an exciting tale. The difference is the same as that between a single incident and the string of incidents that go to make up a short story or novel. A book describing the scaling of a Himalayan peak would simply be the extension or elaboration of an account of that moment when the small party of mountain climbers stood alone on the peak.

In both varieties, the emphasis is on re-creating, as realistically as possible, the actual events—and this means utilizing fictional devices. Of course this can pose a problem for you if you are not adept at the special talents required for writing fiction. It is not a simple matter to master the art of handling dialogue, transitions, realistic yet dramatic descriptions of locale, a sense of pace, and a knowledge of how to milk each scene and episode for its maximum dramatic impact. But these are skills that can be mastered and that, for this kind of article, are essential.

But isn't this "writing fictionally" falsifying the truth, you ask?

To a certain extent, perhaps, but the alternative is to bore the reader. Besides, as the writer you always stick to the truth *as you know it*. After all, you are usually confronted with a subject who, in telling his or her story as it happened, tells the climax first, omits necessary details needed for an understanding of the situation, talks around the subject, hems and haws, and in general deflates the story completely before he or she is finished.

It is your task to take this raw material and give it shape and impact. Once you have in mind precisely what happened, you may proceed to re-create the happening as excitingly as you can, using your insight and imagination to portray the scene as it probably took place. When you have finished, if you have done your job well, your account will probably be closer to the truth than the account wrung from the person who really was there.

The last variant within this category is that article made up of a collection of incidents, each of which bears upon a central issue or theme.

An article stressing the dangers of accepting hitchhikers might begin with a dramatic account of a middle-aged driver picking up a young man, who thereupon pulls a knife and steals the driver's car and his wallet. You could go on to draw the obvious conclusion, buttressing your contention still further with other incidents, all suitably dramatic, and concluding the piece with a recapitulization of the dangers of picking up hitchhikers. Typical examples taken from newspapers and public records could be used to form the basis of cited incidents. The experiences of a famous fire-fighter, flyer, hunter, or explorer could be presented in this way as well. The article would open with a dramatic scene culled from the subject's experiences to be followed with background materials, after which the article would continue on with other exciting scenes dramatized by the writer, based, of course, on the actual experiences. All the action would be tied together *to make a particular point* about the profession or livelihood under discussion or about our own troubled society in general.

Only roughly in the same category would be those articles which rely on the writer's own experiences or confessions—some serious, some humorous, but all written with the purpose of making some specific point by highlighting one's personal experiences. *Fate Is the Hunter* by Ernest K. Gann is a nearly perfect example of this type. The market for this kind of article is huge. *Reader's Digest* is the most famous market for personal experience anecdotes or stories that make a more sentimental point; while the opposite pole in terms of market would have to be the action-adventure magazines, which concentrate, for the most part, on rugged outdoor adventures featuring the spectacular in locale and action. The size and extent of this market can only be adequately estimated by looking over your local newsstand at the range of titles on display. This field is constantly expanding, so that it remains a voracious, demanding market for the writer who can instill real excitement and menace into any of the three varieties of articles mentioned in this category.

In summing up, the basic appeal of the narrative type is its promise of adventure; adventure that can take place either on a city street, or on a lonely farm, or high on a mountaintop in a distant land, with the writer delivering on this promise by providing an exciting yarn told convincingly and in harrowing detail.

Self-help

The self-help or self-improvement articles and books are directed at those people who want to improve themselves physically, emotionally, or financially.

Here are some typical book titles: *How to Build a Second Fortune in Your Spare Time*, *Borrow Your Way to Wealth*, *How to Win Friends and Influence People*, *The Power of Positive Thinking*, *Wake Up and Live.* A glance at the best seller list will usually uncover at least one such book. The most popular of all are the books on health, with dieting leading the way. Right behind the self-help book in popularity is the inspirational book that seeks to tell the reader how to pull himself or herself together in this somewhat unsettling world. Any article or book written to fit the self-improvement category must be written by someone who not only knows how to impart advice, but also has sound advice to give.

Diet or weight reduction is, as indicated above, the most popular subject in the health category. Watch any subway crowd and you will see at once how many people there are who are more than anxious to lose weight. These people are always dieting, always looking for the magic formula that will let them eat all they want and still lose weight. There is no such diet, of course, and fad diets come and go—all promising to do it quickly and painlessly.

If you do have a diet that works, however, and you've checked it out with a physician, you've got a potential gold mine. If you're a doctor to begin with and have a diet that works, close this book right now and contact a publisher.

Handbooks on yoga and other types of physical fitness schemes designed to rebuild flabby muscles and flatten sagging stomachs provide another article field, with the spate of articles and books on isometrics a while back a case in point. If you can tell your reader how to relax and find inner peace at the same time, you're in business.

The books of Adelle Davis have been landmarks in the field of nutrition and have made publishing history, but Mrs. Davis is a nutritionist who knows what she is talking about. Dr. Jarvis's *Arthritis and Folk Medicine* of a few years back, however, had only momentary fame until the FDA moved in. It is best, therefore, for you to be an expert in whatever field you intend to cover. However, if you have stopped smoking and are sure you know how you managed it, you may very well be enough of an expert to create a fast-selling book on the subject, if you can write readable prose.

Some of the most popular books designed to improve the emotional health of the reader have been those that combined both religion and psychology. One of the earliest of such books was Trine's *In Tune with the Infinite*, written in 1897. Then Emmet Fox began writing books on the use of prayer and other religious techniques for self improvement, and the rush was on. *The Power of Positive Thinking* by Norman Vincent Peale is still selling well after years on the market.

Books and articles on the power of simply believing, or on the art of conditioning or hypnotizing oneself to believe, will continue to sell as long as the need to believe in something better for oneself continues to be a dominant human characteristic.

Articles and books dealing with finances usually tell the reader how to invest profitably in the stock market or in real estate. The bulk of the article or book is usually composed of the writer's experience in doubling or tripling his or her own money by utilizing the precepts and techniques described in the book. Illustrative examples abound. How to open your own business, or do better in what business you already own, are also good topics.

If, therefore, you have succeeded in doing something unusual and doing it well; if you have lost weight with a special diet you conceived; if you have made a killing in the stock market or know of someone who has; if you have been transformed by a new outlook on life that made you successful and happy; if your love life has taken a spectacular lift as a result of new techniques you found inscribed on an Eastern temple; if you think you can teach people how to think more positively or live fuller lives — then you should write the self-help book or article.

Again, you must know your subject. You must have something valuable to offer. Even if your methods have been enormously successful with you, you had better be able to show or cite the experiences of others who have also been helped. Some standing in your profession, an academic degree to establish your credentials, or some title, such as Reverend if you are writing in the religious field, are all very important to the validity and credibility of your book or article. However, a lack of such credentials should not stop you if what you have to offer has apparent value and your writing is good enough to fire the enthusiasm of the reader.

The readers of these self-help articles and books are not likely to be too sophisticated intellectually, and they like what is known as a *fast read*: prose that moves along at a fairly brisk pace. This requires short sentences, short paragraphs, and plenty of case histories for the reader to relate to.

The case histories should be interesting in their own right and should demonstrate the general theme or serve as an example of the employment of some particular technique. The more people you can show who have been transformed or made happier or richer with your methods, the better, since these case histories will be the proof of the pudding you have to offer; they must make the reader want to jump up and do likewise.

How-to-do-it

This book you are now reading is a how-to-do-it book. Articles or books telling how to do or build anything, from growing mushrooms in your cellar to building your own helicopter, fall into this category. And don't forget that cookbook in the kitchen.

Everyone wants to make or build things they haven't made or built before. Do they want to learn how to play winning chess? There's a book on it for them. Bridge? Of course. Tennis? Sex? Marriage? Divorce? Tree pruning? Plumbing? Whatever it is that some humans find themselves doing, others want to know how to do as well.

The article or book that fits the how-to-do-it category must be written by someone who knows how to do or build something at least as well as—and preferably better than—the average. He or she then becomes a teacher-writer who painstakingly takes the reader along, step by step, to the completion of whatever task the reader is seeking to accomplish.

In the short how-to-do-it article, you, the writer, are the living example, the chief case history. Have you taught a child to swim this past summer? Have you baked the cake that won the prize at the county fair? Have you found a new spouse while still encumbered with two anxious toddlers? Have you redone the attic to turn it into a rumpus room? Whatever you have done successfully can become the subject of an article or book. Photographs showing you paddling the boat you built or refinishing the old dresser make it more convincing.

As in the self-improvement articles, the prose demanded in the how-to-do-it articles is simple, straightforward, lucid. Short, unadorned sentences are at a premium. You are not trying to impress; rather, you are explaining something quite carefully. But you will notice, when you attempt this kind of article, that it is sometimes very difficult indeed to describe in simple and lucid prose how to do even the most straightforward tasks.

For you must leave out nothing, including the materials you use. Think of that cookbook. As the writer you must start with the ingredients. Your measurements and timings must be exact. You must leave nothing to chance—unless it be the skill of your reader. You must take the reader all the way to the finished product so that he or she knows what to expect.

In summary, the market is there—but very large and filled with all sorts and sizes. A thorough study of this market will be necessary before you, as a beginning writer, can make any intelligent appraisal as to which kind of article you should begin writing. The principal factor in making this choice should be interest. You are always better off when you ally your efforts as a writer with your interests as a person.

Putting This Chapter to Work for You

1. Bring to class a collection of at least five news items, along with your thoughts on the kinds of news features you could write from them. Since presumably others in the class will have done the same thing, swap news items to obtain those that interest you. Then file them for quick future reference.
2. Select the kind of article you like to read or feel you could write comfortably, examine the market for this type of article, and make a determination as to whether or not you would like to write this sort of article. Discuss this choice in terms of your interests. This is an important decision.
3. Repair to the library and research the magazines that you know publish the type of article you have decided to write. Find out as much as you can about each of the magazines you list, including the names of the editors and their requirements in terms of length and tone. For this assignment you should either subscribe to or get hold of *The Writer, Writer's Digest*, and especially the hardbound annual, *Writer's Market*.

chapter five
But What Does It All Mean?

Before anything can happen, the writer must first have something to say—and know what that something is. A simple truth, but sometimes overlooked by the writer with a deadline, anxious to get some words down on paper.

Unless you know precisely what the significance of your article is, your reader won't know either—or care. It is surprising how often this need for a theme—clearly articulated in the mind of the writer—is overlooked.

Let us say that having decided to write an article on the local papermill, a young writer visited the mill and began looking around. Perhaps she was taken on a tour and noticed processes and procedures that excited her curiosity. She was given literature, piles of it, concerning the function of the plant, its facilities, production goals, etc. And then she was ushered into the office of the fellow in charge of public relations for the plant and asked if she had any questions.

By this time, our writer's head is swimming with details. She had a vague idea to begin with as to just how she would approach this article, and some idea of the questions she would ask. But now that she has the opportunity to ask questions, she finds herself asking meager, flat, uninteresting ones, and when at last she leaves the mill and gets back to her desk to sort out her impressions, she's more confused than when she started out that day.

Why Theme Is Necessary

That hypothetical case presented above is why a theme—some call it the central idea—is so necessary. Without a theme you will not know which facts to look for, which facts to play down, what questions to ask, and then, after you have gathered your facts, how to shape and present what material you do collect in a unified and hard-hitting article.

This theme is what keeps you on the track. It gives direction to your inquiries, points to your questions. Otherwise you will flounder aimlessly in gathering material, wasting precious time as a result; and when you do begin to write you will find yourself cutting, slashing, and revising, endlessly and purposelessly. In the end, what you will come up with is a bland, uninteresting collection of useless facts.

How to Make Use of Your Theme

Think of theme as a single statement of fact, that is, a sentence complete with subject and predicate—not a single word, nor a vague idea of what you're looking for and hope to find. It is crucial that you understand the difference between a sentence and a few words that might sound meaningful, but be worth absolutely nothing as a theme.

Let's go back to that hypothetical writer we had ramming

around the papermill. Her idea, let us say, was to investigate or find out just what a large and important industry this was, tucked away in the foothills by a lovely stream. Well, it was large all right, and it was important, and all of her material certainly bolstered that fact—but so what?

Now let's suppose that, before going to that papermill, the writer had made inquiries and had discovered that this particular mill was a prime violator of the pristine cleanliness of the mountain stream it sat beside. With this concern in mind she formulated the following working theme: *Keneebunk Paper Products is violating the Clean Rivers and Streams Act.*

At once, this theme—which may or may not be proven by subsequent investigation—focuses every inquiry, every interview, and is what directs her tour of the plant. She examines the effluent. She examines the water downstream. When closeted with the PR man, the writer asks him bluntly what the mill is doing to prevent further pollution of the stream. Now, when she goes back to her desk and starts looking through the literature handed to her, she is able to pick it apart and examine it in the light of her theme.

It may turn out that the mill is not violating federal standards and is not only in compliance with the new laws governing pollution, but is even going further than other papermills in this regard. As a result, the writer promptly changes her theme: *Keneebunk Paper Products is leading the paper industry in cleaning up its operation.*

The writer had to change her theme in midstream. But the fact that she had a workable theme to begin with is the essential point. With it, she had direction in her research, her interviews, her inspection of the plant. But this is not all. Her newly revised theme continues to be a vital aid when she sits down to write her article.

For she will find that—with her theme always clearly in mind—she will need to do much less revision, and what revision is needed will be done with relative speed and lack of hesitation. Out goes any fact or observation not needed to bolster the central idea. No need to worry about this paragraph or that one, or whether this interesting fact should be included or left out. She simply keeps what she needs to illustrate her theme and discards the rest.

The result will be an article that says what she wants it to say, and says it cleanly, succinctly, and forcefully.

Formulating Your Theme

The trouble with a theme is that you don't always have one when you need it, and until you generate it, you will have great difficulty in proceeding with your article. For, I repeat, until you know what you are trying to say, how can you possibly go about gathering the material needed to say it effectively? The answer, of course, is that you can't.

The solution to this seeming dilemma lies in preliminary research on the topic you are considering. Failing that, an already active interest in the subject will serve the same purpose. This interest or preliminary research will give you the insight you need into the topic's various problems and possibilities.

Thus, to return to our hypothetical writer and her papermill, an interest on her part in the papermill's flouting of pollution laws and also, of course, a study of just what those laws were, gave her the direction needed to provide her with a working theme.

No Propaganda Please

As long as you have a theme in mind when you begin the task of researching your article, you will find yourself able to proceed with a reasonable degree of ease. But it should be made abundantly clear at this point that having a theme or central idea is the main thing, not sticking to it fanatically when the direction of your research and interviewing indicates a different theme emerging.

You must be flexible in this matter. You must not bend facts to suit a preconceived notion in order to stick to your theme. Theme must be a complement to the facts, needed to charge them with significance — any other use of theme is simply a distortion. Worse, it is propaganda.

You are not writing a tract; you are writing an informative article. Always remember that.

To summarize, before writing anything — be it a story, a novel, or an article — you must have some theme to guide you in the selection and rejection of your material. You may change this theme in the process of writing, but without a central idea to guide you, no unified article can be accomplished, and what writing is managed will be brutally difficult.

Putting This Chapter to Work for You

1. Look over those news items you brought into class earlier. For each one postulate a news feature, complete with theme, based on the contents of the news item.

2. Theme is a statement. It is not necessarily a profound statement. In non-fiction, it is enough simply to sum up what a

collection of facts points to most obviously. Find the theme of any four articles in the field you should be now actively investigating as a possible market for your own work.

A good method would be to check out the banner caption under the title as a statement of the article's theme; then read the article to see if the caption is the theme. Some articles will not have such a caption, but the title should serve as an excellent clue in either case.

chapter six
Who's Talking Here, Anyway?

With the advent of so-called New Journalism and the cassette recorder, the writing of non-fiction has opened up considerably. Now the writer can introduce himself or herself more readily into his or her articles, take personal stands, and in a sense participate in the world of events he or she is reporting. In addition, the cassette has made the interview a subtle exercise in mental fencing, often with more revealed by the subject than he or she might have intended.

This chapter discusses non-fiction writing in terms of point-of-view.

Nuts and Bolts

Let's assume you have decided to do a feature story on the local zoo. You have done some preliminary investigation and your theme for now is: *Our zoos are terrible prisons for wild creatures.* The vantage point from which to discuss or relate your findings to the reader could be that of the average citizen, first person singular:

I relented last Sunday afternoon and consented to take my seven-year-old to the zoo. I wish I hadn't. The little boy was fine; and the animals did their best as they paced their tiny cells, scratched their matted fur, and peered out emptily through the bars. But the pervading sense of oppression, the dinginess, and most demoralizing of all, the smell of confined animals made me a very ashamed father as I kept moving, the tiny palm of my son enclosed in my sweaty hand.

The questions he asked were not too easy to answer. The result was that the following day I returned to the zoo to ask a few questions of my own. And what I found out about its management and its financial plight angered and appalled me. In 1964 the budget for the . . .

Or the point-of-view could be simply that of the objective gatherer of information:

Few people, it seems, ever wonder what happens to the Bengal tiger when he finds himself bedded down in their local zoo. Or the Serengeti lion after leaving the baked grasslands of Africa to make his home in a seven-by-ten cage in the midst of one of our cities. It is something few if any wondered about until recently when a few citizens in Des Moines got together to form a group dedicated to finding out—and then doing something about it.

What this group found out was that most zoos in the smaller cities of America are nothing less than animal slums, where near-starvation, disease, filthy cages, and general abandonment are the order of the day. This, at least, is what John Phillips Canterman, the Des Moines headmaster who spearheaded the . . .

Or the point-of-view could simply be that of the interviewer:

Mr. Paul E. Zoss, curator of the Des Moines Animal Garden, a short, powerfully built man in his late forties, has just been kind enough to take me on a tour of the zoo that has been under his care now for almost ten years. He was perspiring slightly, but still obviously enthusiastic as he settled behind his unpretentious desk and leaned back to continue our discussion.

INTERVIEWER: Why did you decide to become a curator, Mr. Zoss?

ZOSS: Well, the job came up, and I'd always liked animals and zoos. I loved to visit the zoo when I was a kid. I guess everyone loves zoos, don't you? It's like having a circus in your own backyard.

INTERVIEWER: Yes, That's true. Where did you take your degree, Mr. Zoss? I assume your profession is that of naturalist.

ZOSS: Yes. Well, I've always wanted to go back to college and take a few courses, but I leave all that sort of thing to my assistant. He's got a string of degrees as long as that python we watched. Me, I'm just the organizer.

INTERVIEWER: I see. Your animals seem to be in need of more room, Mr. Zoss. There were three lions in that one cage, and they seemed terribly crowded—and ugly.

ZOSS: We are a little short of space. That closed off wing you asked about used to be our lion house, but it's in pretty bad shape and the bars were actually getting loose in the concrete. I've been after the mayor for some money to reopen it, but you know how tight things are nowadays.

INTERVIEWER: I certainly do. Could this be the reason for the condition of the Polar Bear tank? If you will remember, it...

In all three examples, though the theme was the same, the vantage point from which the article was written was different. In the first, the writer was a committed and disturbed individual seeking answers for personal reasons. In the second, he was the objective reporter who came upon an interesting, if depressing, story and told it as completely and objectively as he could. In the final illustration, the writer decided to sit back and let an official tell his story, content to let the theme emerge between the lines.

Which Point-of-View to Choose

Practically, which point of view to choose depends on your situation vis-à-vis the material. If you live near your story, or the establishment or individual or industry you consider newsworthy, you can, if you wish, make your article an outgrowth of a visit and simply relate that visit to your reader.

If, as you visit the establishment and pick up your impressions and literature, you find that the best way to capture the significance of it all is to have an interview with an individual connected with your story—which should always be attempted anyway—then you might decide to shift gears and make that interview the body of your article, as in the last example above.

It would be quite natural, as well, to combine your first-person account of the visit with any interviews you may have been granted. Often the nature of the material you uncover as you research your article will determine, finally, what point-of-view you settle on.

If, on the other hand, you live far from the source of your article, you will have to rely on research and telephone interviews almost exclusively. In this case, the objective, non-involved point-of-view is the best one to use.

The audience for whom you are writing the article—and, closely allied with this factor, the magazine for which you are slanting the article—must also be taken into account when deciding on point-of-view. The personal, first-person viewpoint is ideal if you are writing an article in which you want your reader to identify with you, and is a fine choice, not only for the less formal how-to-do-it articles, but also for travel articles and adventure or hunting and fishing articles—those in which you are mixing fact as well as personal experiences.

The objective viewpoint is more suitable for the heavier, more prestigious article—a discussion on foreign policy, for instance, or the development of a new die-casting technique in the auto industry for *Fortune*, articles where the writer's personal feelings and experiences are extraneous to the issues discussed, and in which massive research and acute analysis are the most important elements in the article.

In the final analysis, the choice of the best point-of-view is something that can only be determined by how effectively the one you select enables you to say what you want to say. And that, as you must know by now, is determined by your theme.

To summarize, the viewpoint can be that of first person, with the writer actively involved in the material and events of the article he or she is writing. Or it can be that of an objective gatherer of information presenting the facts as interestingly as possible without ever venturing on stage. Or the writer can step back and become simply an interviewer, allowing the subject to give the reader the facts as they are revealed by his answers to the writer's questions—a method that need not be restricted to the interviewing of celebrities. Which point-of-view to select depends not only on the writer's location vis-à-vis his or her material—both in place and time—but on which viewpoint best accomplishes the development of the theme.

Questions for Study and Discussion

1. Bring in for class discussion and examination an example of each of the three viewpoints used in presenting material.
2. Examine *Scientific American* and *Fortune* magazines for examples of the objective point-of-view.
3. How many examples of the personal, first-person approach beyond the leisure and service magazines (*Mechanics Illustrated, Popular Science, Sports Afield, True, Hot Rod,* etc.) can you find? Do you think this approach to a subject is as valid as the older, more rigidly adhered to, objective form of presentation?

Putting This Chapter to Work for You

Decide which point-of-view you would like to use on the news feature you are—or should be—preparing from one of those news items. You decided on your theme the last time. Remember?

chapter seven

Please... You're Putting Me to Sleep

You've heard it often enough, I'm sure. Your style is you. It is not something you can graft onto your writing. It's there all the time. Well, that's true, of course. But there is just the chance that if your style is you, trouble could still be brewing—because sometimes you are a bore. This chapter on style, then, will be an attempt to help you write without either confusing your reader unduly or putting him or her to sleep.

Unlike the writer of fiction, the non-fiction writer has no spectacular plot developments, no adroit characterizations, no climactic denouement to make a dreary style finally bearable. Though as a non-fiction writer, you also must entertain your reader, entertainment is not your sole responsibility to the reader. The non-fiction writer must also inform.

The problem then becomes one of how to inform without becoming didactic, without haranguing. Without boring. Surely you've suffered at times in the hands of a dull teacher, someone who knew the subject perfectly but imparted it with all the lightness and grace of a politician's response. One of the few tools you have as a writer of non-fiction to avoid this sort of thing is your style.

It is not the business of this text to take upon itself the task of changing your style—or to make it an imitation of some other writer. All this chapter can do is to help you make *your* style say clearly and forcefully whatever it is you wish to say.

With this in mind, let's go over a few concepts you might keep in mind as you write.

Flatness in Your Style

As you go over your work—hunting for the misspellings and grammatical errors—you may very well notice that passages you had hoped would sound exciting and informative, sounded instead curiously flat, despite what you had thought was exciting material.

Flatness in writing is the result of a lack of emphasis. Usually this happens when the writer, anxious to get the facts straight and not thinking in terms of style, simply lists items, facts, quotations, and so on without noticing that he is constructing sentences with little or no assignment of priority as to the relative importance of one idea over another:

> Clifford Beers was haunted by a fear that he would be afflicted with epilepsy. This same disease afflicted his brother. Yet he managed to struggle through his studies and obtained his degree from Yale University in 1897. He worked in a tax collector's office and a life insurance company during the following three years. In 1900 he developed a severe depression with persecutory delusions. His despair became acute. He attempted suicide by jumping from a fourth-floor bedroom window. He was seriously injured. But he recovered from the fall within a few months.

Now let's read that same passage with the sentences reconstructed to emphasize certain elements in place of others:

Even though Clifford Beers was continually haunted by a fear that the same disease afflicting his brother—epilepsy—would soon attack him, he managed, nevertheless, to struggle through his studies and obtain his degree from Yale University in 1897. During the following three years he worked in a tax collector's office and a life insurance company, but in 1900 developed a severe depression with persecutory delusions. His despair became so acute that he attempted suicide by jumping from a fourth-floor bedroom window. Though seriously injured, he recovered from the fall within a few months.

Notice how sentences were combined with others to form dependent clauses or parenthetical expressions, while the important elements were given the status of independent clauses—statements that could stand by themselves:

FROM: He was haunted by a fear that he would be afflicted with epilepsy. This same disease had afflicted his brother. Yet he managed to struggle through his studies and obtain his degree in 1897.

TO: Even though Clifford Beers was continually haunted by a fear that the same disease afflicting his brother—epilepsy—would soon attack him, he managed, nevertheless, to struggle through his studies and obtain his degree from Yale University in 1897.

The rationale for this priority is obvious: the important fact that needs emphasis is Beers' strength of character in persisting in his studies despite the neurotic dread of epilepsy that dogged him throughout the four years. With this in mind, the impressive fact of his graduation *despite this near-disabling phobia* is stated in an independent clause, and is kept until the end of the sentence so that it will remain more clearly in the reader's mind. The principle employed here is that what comes last or first in a sentence is, by that very fact, emphasized.

UNEMPHATIC:
   While Chekhov was the principal support of his family, he attended medical school and wrote short stories.

If your desire is to emphasize the fact of Chekhov's Herculean labors on behalf of his family, you can emphasize this point by placing it at the end of the sentence:

EMPHATIC:
>   While attending medical school and writing short stories, Chekhov was the principal support of his family.

Periodic sentences in place of loose sentences also make for a more emphatic prose style:

LOOSE:
>   There will always be war as long as we perceive our fellow human beings as essentially fearsome and untrustworthy and hateful.

PERIODIC:
>   As long as we perceive our fellow human beings as essentially fearsome, untrustworthy, and hateful, there will always be war.

The obvious advantage of periodic sentences in terms of emphasis should not outweigh, at times, the need for a certain looseness or casualness of style. If every sentence is so constructed as to always emphasize the most significant point the sentence is making, a certain straining for effect will be apparent to the reader. The prose will become rather wearying as a result. Keep your periodic sentences in readiness then for your high points, when you wish to nail down your most crucial elements.

In other words, when you reconstruct your sentences to impart emphasis—whether it be by placing important elements at the beginning or at the end of the sentence, or by arranging ideas periodically in the order of climax—you should know precisely what effect you intend. It may seem artificial and terribly time-consuming, but it is this effort that gives professional polish to your writing.

But again, go easy. Not every sentence should be emphatic. How would you like to have someone shouting at you all the time, eyes wild with excitement, face contorted in a fever of anxiety over the death of a rabbit?

Variety in Sentence Structure

A lack of variety in the structure of sentences is like listening to someone who talks for a long while without expression. There is no rise, no fall in tone—just a steady monotone. This comes of constructing sentences that have a distressing sameness both in type and length.

A style in which all sentences are of a moderate length is bad;

one in which all sentences are short and choppy is also undesirable. The cure is to vary the length and kind of sentences you employ. Parenthetical devices—the dash, the comma—can be used to enclose material that might otherwise require still another short sentence. Turn an occasional sentence into a participial phrase. Combine sentence elements. But once again, don't forget to let a few simple sentences stand as they are for balance.

Let's go back to the story of Clifford Beers:

> Beers' mental disorder persisted. He was placed in a mental hospital and diagnosed as a manic-depressive. Beers decided to reform the institution and improve conditions during one of his manic states. These activities were greatly resented by the hospital authorities. As a result he was put in a strait-jacket at one point for 15 hours. He was transferred soon after to another hospital. There, his attempts to reform the place were rewarded with 14 weeks of confinement in a violent ward. However, he continued his crusade. He wrote letters to public officials on every scrap of paper he could find. One of these letters reached the governor of the state. This letter actually brought some improvements in the institution.

The problem in the above passage is primarily that of a lack of variety in sentence type. Almost all of the sentences are short and choppy as well. A change, then, in both the length and type of sentence employed, should bring some improvement:

> Beers' mental disorder persisted, however. Soon he was placed in a mental hospital and diagnosed as a manic-depressive. It was during one of his manic states that Beers decided to reform the institution and improve conditions. But these activities were greatly resented by the hospital authorities and at one point he was placed in a strait-jacket for 15 hours. Soon after, he was transferred to another hospital, where his attempts at reform were rewarded with 14 weeks of confinement in a violent ward. However, he continued his crusade, writing letters to public officials on every scrap of paper he could find; and when one of those letters reached the governor of the state, it actually brought some improvements in the institution.

The rewritten passage still contains simple sentences, and a short one as well. All of the sentences are definitely not of the same length—nor of the same construction—and that seems to make the difference. In more than one case, sentences were combined to form compound sentences, and in other cases, sentences were transformed into dependent clauses:

> FROM: However, he continued his crusade. He wrote letters to public officials on every scrap of paper he could find. One of these letters reached the governor of the state. This letter actually brought some improvements in the institution.
>
> TO: However, he continued his crusade, writing letters to public officials on every scrap of paper he could find; and when one of these letters reached the governor of the state, it actually brought some improvements in the institution.

Another bonus gained when one varies both the type and length of sentences is what is known in editorial circles as the fast read. As mentioned earlier, lengthier sentences have a tendency to pull the reader along—*when they are well constructed.* If you will read over the first versions of both sample passages, you should notice how choppy they are and how much more slowly each of them reads as a result.

And here's good news: once in a while you may start a few sentences with those heretofore forbidden beginners: *but, because, and, or, nor, for, yet.* In fact, there is no word in the English language you may not start a sentence with—just do it correctly.

Consider also the variety you can achieve by starting occasionally with a prepositional phrase or a verbal. Beginning with an expletive like *there* or *it* will also help, as will starting off with an adverbial clause or a conjunction. Variety can also be achieved by changing the usual subject-verb-object pattern of your sentences and by mixing the usual declarative sentence with a question every now and then. And don't forget the imperative sentence.

Circumlocution

The habit of taking the long way around to say something can well-nigh ruin your ability to say clearly what you have in mind. Though you may regard this as your own particular "style" of writing, you should try to get over this habit, since it is generally agreed by all authorities (and readers) that circumlocution not only bores, it offends.

Perhaps you are not aware that you make this error in your writing; but if you do not, you are perhaps the only living writer who doesn't. Most first drafts are filled with this clutter of excess verbiage, designed, usually, to impress. That is why the writer revises, cuts, slashes, combines, refines. Saying it your way may not necessarily be saying it clearly or directly.

Notice how much fat we can trim off the next examples.

FROM: I dislike the practice of making a profitable business out of college athletics from the standpoint that it has a detrimental and harmful influence on the college students, and, to a certain degree and extent, on the colleges and universities themselves.

TO: I dislike commercialism in college athletics because it is detrimental to the students and even to the universities themselves.

FROM: The council president asserted the danger was from unguarded machines, which may lessen the usefulness of workers in later endeavors as well as reduce their life expectancy.

TO: The council president said that unguarded machines may severely injure or kill workers.

That last example brings to mind the suspicion that most people who habitually practice circumlocution are fundamentally dishonest. They are trying not to be clear. Their purpose is to deceive, to cloak their behavior. Listen to a politician on a question and answer program on television. Read carefully the pronouncements that come from Washington on anything from prices to foreign policy and note how consistently deception, not clarity, is the rule, with circumlocution, not directness, the method.

A decent respect for the intelligence and maturity of your reader will help you to avoid the habit of circumlocution.

Another way to tighten up your style is to simplify wherever you can by reducing clauses to phrases, and phrases, in turn, to single words. Here are some examples:

FROM: He is handsome in appearance, but he is a rather selfish person.
TO: He is handsome, but rather selfish.

FROM: When the time to go had arrived, Anna picked up

her suitcase and went to the door.
TO: When it was time to go, Anna picked up her suitcase and went to the door.

In short, never use several words where a single one will do. Watch out for:

in this day and age (today)
call up on the telephone (phone)
destroyed by fire (burned)
was made the recipient of (given)

Naturally, not all writing has to be simple. Highly complex or technical subjects at times call for complex and technical language. But don't ever be ashamed to express a simple idea in simple language. In fact, you should be ashamed when you find you cannot do so. Complicated language is not an indication of superior intelligence. On the contrary, it often reveals at best a lazy mind; at worst, a dishonest one.

Unintelligibility

Unintelligibility is close to circumlocution in its effect, but its cause is not usually the desire to impress or obfuscate, but rather the writer's own feeble grasp on just what it is he or she is trying to say. The writer's own lack of comprehension is simply reflected in the unintelligibility of what he or she writes:

Faith and love as being intangible, they only exist if we wish to believe in them, thus it takes a strong desire to want to care, for something, and that it must be cherished, cared for, worried about and watched over, is for it to become unique.

For one thing this should be three sentences, not one—and this writer should have known that, at least. Let's revise for clarity and see what emerges from that muddle:

Faith and love are intangible qualities. They can only exist if we believe in them. Thus it takes a strong desire to make us care for something—desire and effort; for before what we cherish can become unique in our eyes, it must first be cared for, worried about, and watched over.

This might have been what that writer had in mind. And then again, of course, this revision may be totally wrong, missing entirely the point the writer wished to make. Yet what choice has the reader but to revise as he or she reads? And what a labor it is to puzzle through such confused and illogical prose.

Many would-be writers assume that to clear up this kind of prose is precisely what editors are hired to do. They confidently think that taking the time to clarify their meaning is beneath them — is quibbling over nonessentials.

This is not true. As soon as an editor reads that kind of writing, he knows without further ado that his intelligence is being insulted and his time wasted — that the writer has not even taken the time to read over his own work and make himself clear. If the writer doesn't care, neither does the editor.

The manuscript is promptly sent back to the writer.

Paragraphing

How long, you must have found yourself wondering in the past, should a proper paragraph be?

The answer is: Any length you want, from one word to three pages of closely packed sentences. It depends on you, on your needs and designs as a writer. Neither extreme is the rule, and today we find that most writers keep their paragraphs reasonably short. If they don't, the magazine's editor will break up the text anyway to suit his idea of what looks right for his pages. Solid blocks of type are seemingly too forbidding an aspect for today's readers.

Sometimes, while reading over your article, you will find that some of your paragraphs will seem unduly skimpy, others too drawn out, and still others filled with a scattering of ideas, none of them going anywhere.

The first thing to remember is that a paragraph should be regarded by the careful writer as an entity in itself, one that — like a sentence — has its own rules and its own form. This means that each paragraph must make a point, and within each paragraph — either at the beginning, the middle or the end — that point must be stated clearly, with the remainder of the paragraph containing facts designed to bolster that contention.

A paragraph that seems too thin or unconvincing usually turns out, upon examination, to be primarily a collection of assertive statements; but simply saying it is so doesn't always make it so. Though each paragraph must indeed make a statement, it must then go on to contribute the evidence needed to build conviction that this statement is not just bullish assertion.

It is important also to make sure that not all of your paragraphs are of the same length. It might help in this regard to think of short paragraphs as assertive attention-getters, while the longer paragraphs are those in which you follow up the points you made earlier, but this time with solid, unhurried reasoning.

With this last point in mind, you can see why an article consisting almost entirely of short paragraphs borders on the sophomoric, while one that contains massive, interminable paragraphs, with few if any short paragraphs to break up the page, can be as deadly as waiting for a very long freight train to pass.

Finally, the necessity for variety in sentence structure, the need to emphasize certain elements over others in your writing, the problems of circumlocution, and the necessity for knowing and then stating clearly what you have in mind should not and must not be regarded by the writer as matters of little consequence. The professional writer takes pride in his or her skill and delights in adhering to the finer points of style and construction.

Questions for Study and Discussion

1. How often in the past have you had to recast sentences and rework paragraphs in order to insure the readability of your writing? Have you ever felt the lack of such revision as a fault in your writing? How often have teachers complained when you handed in your first, off-the-top-of-your-head draft without revising it? Have you ever wondered about this?

2. Have you ever found that when you did set about reworking your prose, you found that all you succeeded in doing was making it worse? Do you accept this fact as a harbinger of trouble for your career as a writer?

3. Most writers — at one time or another — have had to sit down with a grammar text and puzzle this whole matter of clauses and phrases and sentence structure out for themselves so they could recast sentences and punctuate properly. Do you feel it is something you should do as well?

4. Are you aware that editors will not read manuscripts in which it is obvious the writer does not know how to write grammatically, and that poor spelling is a dead give-away in this regard?

Suggestions for Writing

As a starter, take any news item or topic that interests you and write a short news feature for the local or college newspaper.

Then, rewrite it at least three times, correcting first for circumlocution, then for unintelligibility, and finally for simplicity and directness of style. Bring in all three versions for discussion with your instructor and the other students in your class.

chapter eight
Get the Facts

The professional writer of non-fiction is passionate in his or her devotion to facts. Like a hound on the scent, the writer follows the leads and keeps digging until the story is uncovered. The pursuit of the story is as much a reason for writing as is the love of writing. It would not be stretching the point to say that this ability to stay on the trail is the real difference between the amateur writer and the pro. Now is an excellent time to ask yourself: do you get turned on as you begin to track a story? If you do, if your pulse quickens as the trail gets hotter, you're in the right business.

What follow then are some hints as to how to stay on that trail until you do get the story.

Research is hard work. Though much of your time will be spent in libraries hunched over books, periodicals, and old newspapers, your search seldom ends there. More than likely you will have to get up off your duff and perform a considerable amount of legwork in pursuit of the facts. If one library does not have what you need, you must find one that does—or an authority or a witness. If one witness won't give you or can't give you as clear an account as you need, then you start looking for the other witnesses. You're always on your horse, since no one is going to bring you the information you need to write that article. You—and you alone—will have to go out and get the story.

Sometimes you will chase around for an entire day and be lucky to come up with only one usable anecdote, one fog-clearing fact. But then there are the good days, too, when the people you interview tell you what you need to know and a new angle or a surprising fact drops out of nowhere into your lap. Still, the emphasis is on your ability as a researcher. This is the aspect of writing non-fiction on which you will spend the most time.

The Library

The library is, more often than not, where you will have to begin. And I really mean begin, because I am suggesting at the outset that if you want to get a clear, overall grasp of your subject—be it a manufacturing process, a battle, a national hero, an automobile—the best place to start your search is in the children's section of your library.

Assuming you are reasonably unfamiliar with the topic you are exploring, the encyclopedias and the short, but accurate books on the wealth of subjects found in the children's section can prove to be an excellent jumping off point. From the short accounts in the encyclopedias you can fashion a good working outline. If you are doing research on any historical or contemporary figure, you will find the shelves well-stocked with short, but highly informative biographies, a staple for this age group.

From here you can move out into the rest of the library, and this time with a good running start on your topic. Again, check the encyclopedias, the *Britannica* and the *Americana* first, and after this preamble, get to know—and appreciate—your reference librarian. One of the best ways, incidentally, to show your appreciation is to bother him or her only with difficult research problems. You shouldn't, for instance, ask where to find a book when a card catalogue is handy.

The Card Catalogue

Each card gives the number of the book in reference to the book's location on the library shelf, the full name of the author and his dates, the full title, place of publication, publisher, the date of publication, and the length of the book. Sometimes the card will show the book's table of contents. Since librarians—bless them—cross-index, there will be an author card, a title card, and a subject card. In order to find a particular book, then, you have only to know one of three things, the author, the title, or the subject heading under which the book may be found.

If you have access to the stacks, you may go after the books yourself; if not, you will have to give the book's call number to the librarian so that he or she may get the book for you. Of course, it is to your advantage to be able to search in the stacks yourself, since if the book you want is out, you could then glance through other books on the same subject on the nearby shelves and perhaps come out with a book you had not known existed, but which covers the subject nicely.

This is why it is such a good idea to keep on friendly terms with the librarian. Tell the librarian what you are doing. If he or she learns that you're a writer, and if you appear to be an intelligent, careful researcher, the librarian may well make an exception in your case and let you browse through the stacks to your heart's content.

Your next stop after the card catalogue should be the reference desk and the *Reader's Guide to Periodical Literature*, a work that is all but indispensable to the writer, since it lists all the fiction and non-fiction published in leading periodicals since January 1900. Not only can you use this guide for research, but you can also check it to see if any other magazines have covered the same subject you are contemplating, and if so, to what extent. Articles are listed both by subject and by author.

From that point on, the entire reference section is yours to play with. You will find a wealth of guides and indexes, including a guide to the guides: I. G. Mudge's *Guide to Reference Books*, published by the American Library Association. There are biographical references, business and economic indexes, educational indexes, guides to art and architecture, to fashion, geography, history, literature and language, medicine, music, philosophy and religion, political science and law, psychology and sociology, science and engineering. Furthermore, you will find specialized dictionaries, encyclopedias, and biographies, as well as indexes to whatever publications are put out by various disciplines.

If you want a brief biographical sketch on a noted scientist you are planning on interviewing, for instance, simply consult the biographical reference, *American Men of Science*, which covers the physical, biological, and social sciences. If you do not find the scientist cited in that reference, you can then check the *Biography Index*, which covers the time-span from 1946 to date. This will contain a cumulative index to biographical material in books as well as magazines. If that still yields nothing on this particular individual, check *Who's Who in America*. If you still come up with nothing, now is the time to check with the librarian. He or she will be delighted to help (and discover for you that your man, a native of Scotland, was correctly listed in the *Dictionary of National Biography*, which sketches the lives of prominent persons in Great Britain).

It is obvious that the number and variety of reference tools will present a bewildering array at first, and only through diligent application over a considerable period of time will you become as adept as the best librarians in ferreting out the information you need. But persist you must, since for the writer of non-fiction, this skill is an indispensable tool.

What this means in practice is that you really must get to know your librarian. He or she can acquaint you with sources other than the library, for instance, the interlibrary loan service, which can make any book available if the borrower pays the postage. By writing to any of the libraries that list the book in their catalogues or to the state library, the librarian can obtain the requested material in a few days. Your librarian can reach even farther for you, making available the resources of The Library of Congress, which will send—for a nominal fee—xerox copies of magazines or book pages containing whatever information you may request.

The Special Library

If all this fails, your librarian may consult a catalogue, *Special Library Resources*, which lists the books in about a thousand special libraries that are supported by large manufacturers, associations, and learned and technical societies. Again, if the borrower will pay the postage, the books can often be obtained through the mail. This catalogue also extends to the writer the services of such libraries as the Museum of Modern Art, the Army Medical Library, Massachusetts Institute of Technology, and the Pan American Union.

Unlike the public libraries, these special libraries concentrate on covering one particular subject in depth. An example would be the Engineering Societies Library in New York City, or the Folger Library in Washington D.C., which contains books and other material on the Elizabethan Theater, particularly on William Shakespeare.

The average person is unaware of these non-public but quite well-equipped libraries. But the writer can and must take advantage of such sources, for they are often the source of material that cannot be obtained in any other place. These libraries often contain out-of-print volumes of great value, so rare, in some instances, that they usually cannot be found elsewhere. Some of these libraries do occasionally loan books to public libraries. Almost every one of these special libraries will answer some questions by mail.

Visiting the special libraries can be quite an experience. They are much quieter than the public variety, since there are usually fewer patrons, and you can get the books you want a lot more promptly. In addition, these libraries have most of the usual reference works, such as the *Encyclopædia Britannica*, *Webster's New International Dictionary*, the *Periodical Index*, and current magazines.

Public Relations Offices

The public relations officers of most corporations are eager to provide you with the latest information in their particular field. If, for instance, you are interested in obtaining some background on the computer for an article you are preparing, you might write to or visit the IBM publicity office of any large city. You will most likely be rewarded with armloads of material, perhaps including a history of computers along with useful lists of definitions. Oil companies, steel companies, General Motors, all of these companies and similar other large corporations maintain large, well-staffed public relations offices that are devoted to the task of getting their company's message to the public. It is not lost on the members of these staffs that one of the best and quickest ways to get their message out is to give their information to active writers. It only remains for the writer to use such sources judiciously.

The Government

The government is an almost inexhaustible source of valuable information on just about everything. Simply write to: Superintendent of Documents, U.S. Government Printing Office, Washington, D.C., 20402, and request that your name be placed on their mailing list. It costs nothing. Periodically the printing office will send you lists of currently available government publications, priced from 5 cents on up.

One such government publication that should help the young writer is *A Dictionary of Information Resources in the United States*, a listing of all government-sponsored information resources. These listed sources are valuable because they will often answer questions by phone, mail, or in person.

Thus a call to the local office of the Fish and Wildlife Service would give you the date of the opening of the hunting or fishing season, or a list of what local species are protected or in danger of extinction.

Finally, as long as we are discussing the government's resources, we should mention the National Archives in Washington, D.C. It contains a wealth of information on Americans from colonial days to modern times.

Professional Organizations

The National Society of Interior Designers is an organization whose members are the most experienced and competent practitioners in its field. A member of that organization would be an ideal source for information on any phase of interior design. This is true of any of the other professional organizations, whatever the field. Professional societies demand high standards for membership, and this is the researcher's guarantee that the person being consulted is not an amateur, but an expert.

Newspaper Files

Almost every event of national or international importance in the twentieth century can be found listed in *The New York Times Index*. The writer is thus able to track down any story in the *Times* file that may be located in his library. In addition, using the file as a reference for dates, he may find other stories relating to the event he is researching covered in local papers printed at the same time.

Most newspapers keep files ("The Morgue") on important local persons, places, and organizations. These files can also be consulted and might well furnish valuable information for news features and other articles highlighting local events or celebrities.

Chamber of Commerce

Where a town or city is large enough to have a fairly efficient local chamber of commerce, the writer will find its offices filled with information about the community: its industries, roads, civic enterprises, and plans for the future.

Consular Offices

The writer of travel articles or articles on any aspect of a foreign country will find the consular offices invaluable, since it is the business of these offices to disseminate information concerning their country. The office you contact may also be able to put you in touch with individuals living nearby who might be willing to grant interviews concerning their native country. The information obtained in this manner will, of course, be as favorable as it can be to the country in question, but this need not trouble the writer if he is astute enough to separate fact from propaganda.

The Telephone

When the phone rings, it has to be answered or it won't stop ringing. A letter, on the other hand, can be glanced at and swiftly deposited in the circular file. This is why the phone is far superior to letters and questionnaires when it comes to clarifying or eliciting information from busy people.

If you know the name of the person you want to speak to, simply give him or her a call. If the person cannot speak to you at that moment, set up an appointment with the individual and call later. For hard to get, but absolutely vital information as you near a deadline, the phone call to an expert or a public relations office will be worth the added heft to your phone bill.

Of course this means that the person on the other end of the line is at least uneasy, if not annoyed. A phone call is always an intrusion. The best way to handle this is to tell the person at once who you are and why you need a few facts from him or her at this particular moment.

The implication, either stated or implied, should be that you are well on your way to finishing your article and that what you need now—one way or another—is verification of a few important points, points that the individual you are now talking to would want to clarify. You are now interested in accuracy, and so, you assume, is the person you are calling.

Do not, certainly, state this sort of thing belligerently. Be confident that the individual you are calling is as anxious as you are to get the record straight. Indeed, he should be grateful to you for allowing him to do this. Launch at once into a series of questions —preferably written down beforehand—that will elicit unequivocal responses in the shortest possible time. Then, with your answers in hand, thank your informant and hang up.

The Interview

The telephone interview is obviously limited in effectiveness, and no professional writer can rely on the phone call entirely. The personal interview—after all of the material in the libraries and public relations departments has been absorbed—is quite often the only effective way for you to get the bite of secure, really up-to-date information, to give your article the feel it should have of contemporaneity. This is an incredibly fast-moving world, and today's reader expects on-the-spot statements by people currently engaged in the research or activity under discussion.

Most articles of the type described earlier as news features depend a great deal on the interview, its quality and depth. An article about a local beekeeper who is certain he has a cure for arthritis would have to be built almost entirely on the personal interview, though a certain amount of background information would still be necessary and would have to be provided by the usual methods of research.

The problem for the beginning writer is, usually, that he does not know how to get to the person he needs to interview, especially when often he cannot say that he is employed by a specific magazine or newspaper. It always helps to be able to say, of course, that the article is being prepared for the editors of *Harper's* or *The New Yorker*; and this will certainly open many doors. But in the absence of such a claim, it is indeed difficult to get through to your subject.

Those valuable to your article are certainly going to be busy people—whether they be farmers, itinerant inventors, or big business executives—and you must take this into account when you call to request an interview. But do call. Make your request, always being sure to tell precisely why you feel the interview is needed. If you do not sound unnecessarily shy or deferential, and if you do indeed have a good reason for the interview, you will usually be pleased to find that it will be granted.

If, however, you simply cannot get past the ring of PR people and secretaries that surround our busiest, most active administrators, then you will simply have to see what you can find out by interviewing a member of the public relations staff. If you do a good enough job at that interview—good enough so that the PR person respects your ability—you may be able to go from there to an interview with the individual you're interested in. At the same time, you will undoubtedly be able to gain quite a lot of valuable information from the public relations staff, and you should approach the interview with these people with that conviction in mind. Engaging in an interview with anyone from the

PR staff, with the expressed hope or settled conviction that it is only a preliminary dodge entered into in order to gain finally the interview you really want, will take all the starch out of your interview, in which case you may end up getting precious little of value from either source.

No matter whom you interview, however, you must prepare for it thoroughly. The preparation will be considerably less exacting for an interview with an old prospector who is being interviewed for a personality piece in the local weekly newspaper than for the president of a local college whose innovations in admission policy are causing a stir in academic circles, but some preparation is desirable in each case.

Gather as much background material as you can. As implied earlier, this may be the final stage of your article, in which case you already have a considerable fund of information on the subject and should know almost precisely what it is you are going to ask your interviewee and, even more important, what the general theme or thrust of your questions will be. No matter at what stage of the preparation for your article you may be when you get your interview, you must know as much as you can about the person you are interviewing and the subject under discussion.

Some writers like to sit down before the interview and compose a list of specific questions they want answered along with typical answers, just to get the proper mind set. However you do it, you should enter the interview well primed with good, probing questions.

Before getting down to the meat of the interview, try to lighten the atmosphere with a few pleasantries. As a writer you will be regarded with some awe, just as you in turn will feel somewhat uneasy in the presence of an individual who seems to have accomplished so much in his or her very busy life. If you jump right into the interview, therefore, you will betray this awkwardness and will possibly cut off—at the very outset—any chance you might have had to put your interviewee at ease. On the other hand, don't dawdle. Everyone is busy—or at least is happy to give that impression—so get down to business as soon as it is decently possible.

Questions that invite only negative or affirmative responses can kill an interview. Try to frame your questions in such a manner that while answering, the individual is required to do a certain amount of reminiscing. Try to focus on people as human beings rather than as soulless functionaries. What people think and feel is as important—perhaps more so—than what they do. Try to keep this in mind while at the same time keeping your questions from prying needlessly.

In short, try to establish a rapport with your interviewee that will enable you to know intuitively when you are going too far, or when you are no longer communicating. You must establish this rapport without imposing on your subject unduly. Remember that this individual is giving you his or her most precious commodity—time—in order that you may realize a profit. For that reason—while you should not project yourself as an obsequious fan, anxious to please at all cost—you should respect the individual's time and feelings.

It is extremely difficult at this point to tell you exactly how you should conduct yourself personally. Dress, manners, mannerisms, diction—all are important aspects of the problem, and in today's aggressively informal society, you will have to decide for yourself just how much you will want to defer to the sensibilities of the individual you are interviewing. One rule of thumb only: in general, few people are offended when the person who approaches them is clean and neatly dressed and knows how to smile.

Should you take notes? That depends on you and the person being interviewed. If you have a porous memory, you will have to take some notes. If, on the other hand, you remember what people tell you with precision, you will not need to take as many notes. Some writers bring cassette tape recorders; this practice is rapidly gaining in popularity, despite the often expressed uneasiness this ubiquitous instrument seems to arouse in so many people. For the interview that is going to be nothing but a transcription of questions and replies, the cassette, of course, is a necessity.

For most interviews, you will have to ask the person being interviewed what he prefers. If the recorder bothers him or her, you will simply have to forego its use. It would be a sound practice, therefore, if you mentioned your reliance on the cassette—if such is the case—when you ask or write for the interview.

Even if it is not used during the interview, the cassette can be of great help afterwards. Some writers like to begin dictating the gist of the interview into the recorder as soon as they return to their car or office. In a kind of free association exercise, they get the interview down on tape and then later either type it up or have a paid stenographer do it for them. Reading the transcription of the taped recall in conjunction with the notes taken during the interview can give a pretty fair and accurate distillation of the interview.

Do not, however, allow either your use of the cassette or your diligence in taking notes to intrude unduly on the interview. Note-taking and recording must be done so unobtrusively that the easy give and take does not suffer as a result. Some interviews will require that you take very few notes—except once in a while to nail down important dates or facts—while in other interviews the subject may feel uneasy if he sees you listening blandly while he gives you highly sophisticated and complex data.

In less formal interviews, with people who are not so frantically busy or well-informed on the subject you are pursuing, you may, of course, be a lot less formal with regard to note-taking or using the cassette; but no matter whom you are interviewing, you will get little of value until and unless you are able to relax the respondent.

Consider an interview with an elderly woman concerning her fight to keep her little cottage intact despite the onrushing super highway. You may very well find that as soon as you place your cassette down on the table beside her, the old woman's mouth will suddenly clamp shut as she finds she can't think of a thing to say—except yes or no, and feebly at that.

What do you do? You turn off the cassette and suggest to the old woman that both of you go outside for a walk around the house. You mention that as you drove up you had noticed the garden and the view of the river. Then, during the tour of the grounds, you continue the interview. This time you will probably discover that the woman has no difficulty at all in communicating her love for her house and her fear and apprehension about the proposed highway that threatens to displace it.

The point is that you must do all you can to relax the person you are interviewing. Unless you succeed in this, you will get only the most nominal responses and little of the sidelights and anecdotes so necessary to your article, which should be, in fact, one of the basic purposes of your interview.

In the final analysis, the best way to relax your interviewee is to show yourself to be an intelligent, alert individual, more than casually conversant in subject matter vital to him or her. If you are ill-prepared, halting in your questions, inarticulate on key matters—and if your appearance seems inappropriate in the bargain—you can rest assured that the person you are interviewing will be not only nervous about your presence in his or her home or office, but apprehensive as to the accuracy and justice of the material you will carry forth from the interview.

How long should you stay? A half hour is not as long as you might like; you should try for an hour. That should be all you need in most cases. However long your interview lasts, be sure you can fill it with important, pertinent inquiry and be alert that you do not go over your allotted time, unless it is patently obvious to you that the person you are interviewing desires to continue the session. If you are in rapport with the individual, you should have little difficulty in sensing this.

Under no circumstances, however, should you prolong the interview simply because you yourself are so interested in what you are learning that you want to continue it beyond the agreed upon time-limit, or because you find you still need more material for your article. If, however, you have only one more item to be covered and it can be handled with a brief response, admit this fact, ask your question, then get out. Don't linger at the door. Your time is up. A quick, sincere thank-you is all that is required at this point—along with a request that if you need further information to clarify a few points you may call back. Then git!

What about allowing the person you have interviewed to look over the article before you submit it for publication? Show the interviewee, if you must, any quoted portions that he or she may want to check for accuracy; but do not give the interviewee—or anyone else on his or her staff—a veto on what you write. This is your article and no one else's.

It is not a bad idea, incidentally, to write a brief note of thanks to all of those who helped make the interview possible, and that includes the PR people involved as well as the individual interviewed.

Transcribing the Interview

Transcribe the interview as soon as possible. If you have tape recorded the entire interview, play it back promptly, transcribing from the tape and stopping it every now and then to add visual sidelights you might have noticed in the course of the interview:

> ... that a totally new concept in atomic engineering will have to be considered if we can't lick the problem of waste disposal . . .
>
> (He got up out of his chair and walked over to the window and looked down at the nearly completed power plant, a slight frown on his face. Then he swung back to me, the frown gone.) . . . Of course we will lick the problem. We have to. Our need for cheap power demands . . .

This will set the interview firmly in your mind and give you quite a lift when you begin to write the article.

Notice I suggest you do the transcribing yourself rather than hire a typist, as some writers do. This is important. First of all, as a beginning writer you will not really have the money to hire a typist, and secondly you will find after a few false starts that it is not nearly as difficult as you might have thought to transcribe from tape, especially with the cassettes you can place beside you on the desk.

As alluded to earlier, if you did not use the cassette in the interview, but relied on your notes and your power of recall, you can still use the cassette after the interview. With the battery-powered cassettes you can begin to record impressions of the interview as soon as you reach your car. If you wait until you get back to your hotel room to do this, you can sometimes edit and classify the notes you have taken as you dictate. Reading the notes aloud into the recorder will often jog your memory and material you might have lost if you had waited too long will surface. Then you can relax and return to your home base to transcribe the taped impressions of the interview at your leisure.

Incidentally, don't worry unduly about trying to get a painstakingly accurate, word for word transcription of what your subject said. Almost all recorded conversation must be edited for print, since when people talk they ramble, are careless in their choice of words, and in general are imprecise when they should be specific. As long as you accurately reflect the meaning and import of what your subject said, you are in fine shape. It might be helpful at this juncture to recall what an old reporter friend once told me: if you really want to destroy a public figure, just quote him *word-for-word*.

If you do not like to work with gadgets, as some writers most emphatically do not, you must still — as quickly as possible — do all in your power to get this interview down on paper. Get to your typewriter, read over the notes quickly, then spread them out on the desk around you and begin putting down what you recall of the interview. Rely on your memory and don't dawdle. Keep typing. Use the notes when they are needed to bolster portions of the interview. But above all, keep going. As you write put in as many of the peripheral impressions of the interview as occur to you.

Once the interview has been transcribed in this fashion, glance over it to make sure you haven't left out anything essential. Then put it away in your growing file.

Using Copyrighted Material

Facts cannot be copyrighted. While reading, take notes without copying the exact wording. Jot down only those facts you want to remember. That way you're safe.

Quotations from public speeches may be used freely as can quotations from interviews. Historical and public documents may be quoted freely, even though you read them in a copyrighted book or article. Letters and diaries and historical records are almost certain to be free for the taking. Books and articles old enough for the copyright to have expired may also be used freely; just be certain the work's copyright has not been renewed.

Since opinions come closer to being private property than statements of fact, be wary of restating a person's opinion or interpretation taken from a printed source without proper crediting of that source. In general most publishers have agreed to permit the use of a direct quote from their copyrighted material as long as it is less than fifty words and is properly credited.

To obtain permission for quotes longer than fifty words, all you have to do is write for permission to the owner of the copyright — the author or the publisher. You should be sure to get the permission in writing, however.

What About Pictures?

You can get by as a writer of non-fiction without taking a single picture. Unless you are willing to master what can be a most intricate art, do not decide to concentrate on those markets which demand pictures with their articles. For one thing, these markets are not as interested in the text, usually, as they are in the pictures, which means that your ability to write full and perfectly documented articles will not give you the edge your skill deserves. Furthermore, you will sometimes find, on publication, that your text has been altered considerably in order to make room for the pictures, or worse yet — reduced simply to captions for the pictures.

If you are primarily interested in a career in photo-journalism, you couldn't care less if this happens to your text. But if this is not the case, then I repeat, you should think twice about concentrating on those markets specifying photographs with their articles.

But pictures can help the beginning writer of non-fiction. There are times when a picture can be of such value in illustrating points made in the text — the how-to-do-it article, for instance — that not to have a picture is a real liability. There are many instances where pictures can enhance an article enormously, though the non-fiction free-lancer should keep in mind always that no matter how good his shots might be, if the article is not up to standard, his picture or pictures will not be able to save the situation.

It is, in short, a matter of emphasis. Decide what your skills are and act accordingly. Are you a writer or a photo-journalist? If you are a writer, concentrate on writing the best articles you can —

and if possible get a good picture every now and then when the opportunity arises and when you feel a picture will add a needed something extra.

So then, what kind of camera should you purchase—assuming that you don't already own one you consider adequate. The first thing to remember is not to go overboard on price. Keep your budget under $200. Higher priced cameras are not really simpler to operate. They offer more features to fit more possible uses and as a result require more skill to operate and can be very confusing for the novice. There are cameras today almost as simple to operate as the old box camera that will still give pictures sharp enough for publication.

But do stay away from the cheaper cameras as well, those with plastic lenses, the instant-prints, the drop-in-loads, the odd sizes. Stick with those that have good lenses, use full frame 35mm film, and allow a fair range of control over the shutter speed and lens opening.

Try to purchase a fixed lens automatic exposure camera—with a manual override, if possible—that will focus down to about 3 feet. Where do you find such cameras? This text cannot recommend any specific camera, obviously. Besides, camera technology is changing so rapidly that only general guidelines can be given. What you should do is take your problem to a good camera shop, tell the clerk there what you want from a camera, and allow him to guide you in selection.

One important point: any good, well-stocked camera shop will often have excellent used cameras on hand. Be sure you are dealing with a reliable dealer, one willing to give you some kind of warranty—money back, plus repairs over a reasonable period of time.

Now what about the actual taking of pictures? Obviously, you should search out a good text on the subject and study the many good photography journals on the market. But for now here are a few hints:

Any writer knows intuitively the value of unity and coherence in what he or she writes. The writer must make a point clearly and excise all that does not contribute to that point. The same thing is true of a good picture. It does not just happen, any more than a good feature article does.

If you want to be sure there is nothing in the picture that has no relation to the point that shot is making and that all the elements in your picture do belong, you must do some planning or controlling of those elements that appear in your shot. In other words, you must do some *composing*, just as an artist does when he paints.

The first thing to get rid of is clutter, both in the foreground and in the background. The second thing to do is concentrate on the single most important element in the picture. And for goodness sake, move in close enough to your subject. Of course the photographer must do all this while not appearing to be unduly controlling the content of the picture. The picture must appear to be a natural, realistic shot. In other words, the art is in controlling the elements that show in the picture without appearing to have done so.

Candid shots of accidents, of course, cannot have this much control, but they still must be shot in such a way as to avoid clutter and to concentrate on the important elements. Scenic shots are another problem. You cannot move that mountain peak over so that its rampart is neatly split by those two birch trees, but you *can* move yourself and the camera.

Finally, remember that if a picture is really worth a thousand words, a poor picture is worth nothing. As a writer of non-fiction you must realize that your greatest assets are your abilities to research diligently, to catch the attention of the reader, and to write interestingly and forcefully. Expertise with a camera may well give your articles an added dimension, but you should think of yourself—at least until you have mastered the art of photography—primarily as a writer, one who may on occasion be able to take a good picture when the opportunity offers itself.

To sum up this chapter, research is what makes your articles possible. Without it, little of value can happen, and all you will have to sell is your private, not-too-well-proven assertions. You can get by for a while on personal experiences as long as you bring into the discussions tangible facts and the sense that you are communicating something vital to the reader. But you cannot base an entire career in non-fiction on your own personal experiences— unless of course, like George Plimpton, those experiences are consistently spectacular.

Research can be more challenging than poring over old tomes in dim libraries. Actually, any experience the writer has is valuable: a trip to a mountain retreat, an altercation in a neighborhood bar, a long evening at a school board meeting. Everything is grist.

But that is indeed the brighter side of the coin. More often than not, as a writer of non-fiction you will spend hours hunched over books, interminable hours alone in your car as you drive to an interview, and long evenings plowing through stacks of statistics, pamphlets, self-serving press releases, and company propaganda.

What must sustain you throughout this labor is the knowledge that this process of investigating, taking pictures, gathering material whenever and wherever it can be found is well worth the effort when it results in an exciting, informative, well-written article.

Putting This Chapter to Work for You

1. Choose a contemporary figure—anyone from Marlo Thomas to Henry Kissinger to Kurt Vonnegut—someone so contemporary that your best source of material will be in newspapers, magazines, and newsmagazines, necessitating your consulting first the *Reader's Guide* and then the other guides and indexes, and gather what material you can. From this material construct a profile, starting with a physical description, hopefully while he or she is doing something typical—shooting an elephant, singing, lecturing—that will give a good picture of your subject, while at the same time highlighting those traits that have established his or her fame.

   Go on then to a straightforward account of the vital statistics: birthplace, family, education, early career experience. This should lead into the main body of your paper in which you isolate those elements in your subject's career that have brought him or her to current prominence. If possible, end the profile with a quote from your subject that would tie the profile all together—and perhaps give you your title.

2. Choose a historical figure—anyone from Caesar to Bismarck to Louis Pasteur—and gather material on him or her and write a short profile, similar in form to the profile outlines on a contemporary figure.

3. Choose an older *local* figure—farmer, teacher, store-owner, doctor—and interview him or her on the following topic: what do you think is the biggest change since you were a boy/girl? Using the material gained from the interview, write a short article on what your subject thinks was the biggest change.

4. Interview a few local doctors on the subject of fad diets. You will have to make appointments to see them, of course. But once you tell them your purpose and your topic, they will most likely be glad to give you a few minutes out of their busy day. Before you conduct the interview, you should do some research on the subject of diets. During the interview be sure to ask them what their overriding concern is in relation to fad diets. If they think them dangerous or foolish, why? And finally how do they suggest people lose weight?

   This should give you the basis for an informative article on dieting—a perennial favorite with almost any publication.

part three
THE ACT OF WRITING

From now on, it will be assumed that you are ready to roll up your sleeves and get cracking on a real honest-to-goodness writing project. Those suggested assignments following the last chapter were designed to whet your appetite—and to illustrate somewhat graphically the problems to be overcome in writing even the simplest articles. What follows—hopefully just in time—is a step-by-step approach to a solution of those problems and finally the creation of an article you can confidently send on its way to a waiting editor.

chapter nine
I'd Like to Write About That

A look into yourself is essential if you are to discover the correct field of interest for you as a writer. It will do you little good to chafe at this. Every writer, whether of fiction or non-fiction, is confronted with the problem of finding out what he or she does best. Accordingly, some guidelines for working toward a solution of this dilemma will be suggested in this chapter.

The man who hates his job is not a very conscientious worker—as Detroit is rapidly finding out. Writing is gruelling work. The absence of a time card and a demanding, tyrannical boss makes it almost impossible for the writer to work unless he is in tune with what he is writing. Without this inner willingness, the deadline he sets himself will come and go while he sharpens pencils and postpones that trip to the library.

But even more significant: what the writer finally does write without willingness will not represent him. It will be a tortured amalgam of other influences, of conflicting purposes, and will lack the single indispensable element of all good writing: conviction. In short, even in writing the supposedly more commercial, more crass non-fiction—unless the writer approaches his subject with enthusiasm and respect, what he produces will be worth little.

The lesson is obvious: make a personal inventory of yourself and write from that knowledge.

Your Hobbies

First of all, you must have a hobby. If you are a photographer, fine. Articles on photography find a ready market in the photography magazines, several of which you must be quite familiar with by this time. Or perhaps your hobby is classical music, or rock and roll. Check *Stereo Review* or *Rolling Stone* for the kinds of articles you might write on either of these two subjects. Are you a weekend sailor? Check the boating magazines. A weekend flyer? Check *Flying* or *Private Pilot*. And there are many other magazines, as you must know by now, since you should already have researched the various markets extensively.

Perhaps you are too busy going to school or keeping house to get interested in a hobby. Well then, examine your enthusiasms. What would you like to learn more about? What has always aroused your curiosity whenever it came up in conversation? You say you are a nut about wildlife programs on TV? *Born Free* was your favorite motion picture? Good. So start reading about animals. Start digging deeper than the average reader. Become a kind of expert on the gorilla, for instance. Soon, you will have an extensive library on the subject and will find yourself bursting with material for articles.

But does this mean you stay on this one tack for the rest of your writing career? Of course not. Still, it is a beginning.

Let's suppose you write an article for a flying magazine in which you discuss the difficulty of navigating in foul weather. In the course of your research for that article, you gain considerable expertise on meteorology, and your article shows it. As a result of this bit of research, you now have acquired both a working knowledge and an interest in weather. You examine the magazines dealing with weather and weather forecasting and the trade magazines that deal with meteorology and write an article for one of them, pointing up the need for clearer and less obtuse terminology in the forecast bulletins sent to out-of-the-way airports. Student pilots would appreciate this enormously.

As you begin noticing more and more about weather and how it affects the pilot, you begin to unearth more data about smog and the conditions under which it is produced. Soon you find yourself writing for ecological and farm magazines about the effect of smog on growing things. You discover that smog is not caused primarily by lead in gasoline, and you write an article highlighting this fact for any of the magazines that publish articles on cars. This leads to a new expertise, the problem of refining a gasoline that will not pollute and of building engines that burn fuel more efficiently and completely.

Thus do the ripples of your interest keep expanding—and with it your markets and your career.

Don't Bite Off More Than You Can Chew

If you will notice, following the direction of your interests assumes a slow accretion of material over a span of time. One thing leads to another—naturally. An authoritative grasp of a subject cannot be acquired overnight. There will have to be hours of patient digging, studying, digesting, and writing on the subject.

So what do you do meanwhile? Start slowly by sending articles of modest length to modest magazines as you gather your feet under you. An article on the current state of urban housing for the poor might be a natural for you in terms of interest, since you live in a city that is currently in the throes of what used to be called urban renewal. But can you handle the subject adequately at this stage of your writing career? Not unless you are an official in the city or the building commission and have been wrestling with this subject firsthand for some time. You *can* ease yourself into the subject by doing an unpretentious article on what one family you know has gone through as a result of urban renewal. You can visit the newly constructed apartments and see how the tenants like their new quarters. How well is it working in detail? Uncover the human element so often glossed over by the big planners in Washington and city hall.

In this way you will still be following your interest, but you will be restricting yourself to an aspect of the problem you can handle at this stage. As you continue mining the subject, your expertise will grow. Inevitably it must. With these shorter articles and months of research behind you, then you may write that big article for *Harper's* or *Atlantic* about the mess in urban renewal.

Is It a Researchable Topic?

You won't find out whether your topic is researchable until you have started to do your research, but it can happen that even though you are really turned on about a particular topic, it is just so new that there is very little you can find between the covers of a magazine or book on the subject. However, since you know about the subject, something must have been printed on it somewhere. If all you can find is one skimpy article on the topic, and your interest is so difficult to quench you must find more, write to the author of the article and ask him or her to help you. If he or she shares your enthusiasm, perhaps you can swap information and sources. Then again, the author may not answer your letter.

So what do you do?

Keep your eyes and ears open. Alert your librarian to watch for any new articles or books on the subject. Tell your friends your problem. Pore over book reviews in *The New York Times* and elsewhere and begin building a library on your topic until you find yourself ready to go with your article.

In the meanwhile, turn to other, possibly related, topics for other articles.

How Much Time and Money Can You Afford to Invest on Speculation?

An established writer can usually find out beforehand how much he will receive for an article, since more than likely his query or telephone call to the editor has already settled not only the payment, but the length and main thrust of the article.

But even if the beginner gets a go-ahead for an article, he may find that the expense and time necessary to complete the article will outweigh what he receives in payment.

Recently a writer journeyed to a town some sixty miles distant to interview the parents, acquaintances, and teachers of a baseball star for the purpose of writing an article for a sports magazine, highlighting the hometown's reaction to the ballplayer's fame. The trip and the interviewing, the calls and telegrams to set up the interviews, the time taken to write the article, when computed in terms of dollars and cents, was more than the amount the writer received for the article. As an investment in learning the facts of writing for publication, however, the experience was priceless. But you should ask yourself how much of this kind of experience you can afford. The best solution when this happens is to shrug and keep going—always trying to do better the next time.

More than likely, as you get into your stride, you will find yourself working on more than one article at a time. This means you can be researching two or three possibilities at once, thus spreading the cost of the research for each article. You will find that the research and the interviewing you amassed for one article can serve, with sometimes only a slight modification, as the guts for still another article.

A conservation article on tree farms in the Adirondack Mountains written for a conservation magazine, if researched with enough depth, can leave you with more material for an article on campsites in the region for a trailer magazine, and perhaps a travel feature highlighting the lakes of the region for a travel magazine; the research for all three articles paid for by the first one you wrote.

In choosing your topic then, look to yourself, your hobbies, and your enthusiasms and build on that foundation. Don't worry about this limiting you unduly, for as your knowledge grows, your reach will extend surely into other fields. Keep your initial efforts modest. Don't force it. As a result of that modesty, the first articles you write may be financially unrewarding. But keep going until you get your legs under you.

Putting This Chapter to Work for You

1. Examine yourself—as this chapter suggests. List your hobbies, interests, enthusiasms, in that order. Now list what you know as a result of these hobbies or interests. Next list what you do not know but would like to find out. From either one of these latter lists you may find the topic for your first send-to-the-editor article.
2. Perhaps you are just interested in people. You would like to specialize in interviewing interesting people and telling their story. All right. That's perfectly understandable. But which people should you choose? Where do you find the odd, the fascinating, the exciting people?

    You have already done some interviewing, so now your feet are at least a little wet. Check out the newspaper, especially the local tid-bit sections, for likely subjects. (I recently read a short announcement of a day-long open house held in honor of a woman celebrating her 90th birthday. Imagine

attending that open house and interviewing that woman.)
3. Whatever decision you make concerning a topic, stick to it—and start researching. If you are still having trouble, go back to the first chapter, second part, and reread it, on the lookout for a market that might not have occurred to you. And don't worry: guided by your interests, you should find something you will want to write about.

chapter ten
Dear Editor

Every writer—beginner or professional—starts with a query, since it points him or her at a specific target. Yet unless the writer has a pretty fair idea of what he or she is going to write and also for which magazine, he or she is not yet ready to write that query.

It is assumed that by now you have selected a topic that interests you—either because of previous experience with the material or because you have an active enthusiasm for learning about the field. Fine. But even so, you are not yet ready to write a query.

Before you can write a query, you must do preliminary research, enough to tell you how you plan to handle the topic, what your slant will be, and just how good your sources are. This last is very important. Without adequate source material, you might have a great lead and a snappy close, but little else of substance. No matter how intriguing your query letter may sound, you can't sell a poorly documented article.

Finding the Target

By now you should be market-wise. Select your target magazine and read the contents thoroughly, analytically. If you cannot find a copy of the magazine in the library or the newsstand, consult the writers' magazines mentioned earlier, *The Writer's Digest* or *The Writer*—preferably both. Go through back copies until you find the listing of the editorial requirements for the magazine you have chosen. When you find it, read carefully the editor's stated preferences in terms of theme, length, and so on.

Let us say that by this time you have decided to write about a maverick farmer you know about who has decided to beat the high cost of today's farm machinery by returning to the use of large Belgian workhorses like his father used. You have already looked through the popular farm magazine you bought in the drugstore, but found that it seemed oriented almost entirely to big farm operations where the emphasis is on modern farming practices. Furthermore, the issue was crammed with ads for enormous tractors and combines.

Now, however, in looking through a list of farm publications in the *Writer's Digest* you come across a listing of the *Farmland Times*. You read the editor's comment that he would like to see articles promoting rural and farm life, with the emphasis on nostalgia and strong human interest. The appeal, he says, should be general and down to earth. This looks like the magazine for your article.

Preliminary Research

Accordingly, you visit the farm and talk to the farmer. His name is Dan Benedict, and he is proud of what he is doing, but just a little angry that conditions are such in the dairy industry that he has to consider this alternative. As your casual interview continues, you see that this farmer is also looking upon his return to horse power as a way of bringing back the family farm, with the horses—reminding him of his days on the farm when he was a boy—serving as a symbol of that return to an older, simpler way of life. His eyes light up when he takes you into the barn to show you his four sturdy Belgian mares, their massive flanks still steaming and quivering from the day's work only recently completed.

The interview ends as you get a few specific facts and figures concerning his total farm operation, especially the costs of the horses as opposed to the cost of farm machinery. You find he has already gone a complete year with the horses and he's cut his operating costs by a third. There are a lot more facts you will want later, plus interviews with the entire family, but for now you are set.

You go home to write your query letter.

The Query Letter

The best definition I can think of for the query letter is that it is *a powerful sales pitch addressed to a potential customer—in this case an editor.*

Your letter should catch the editor with a provocative first sentence, then follow with a paragraph telling him what the article is about, mentioning the theme as well. One or two facts and anecdotes should quickly follow to support the premise given earlier, after which the letter should close with a paragraph in which you ask to do the article for the editor and suggest a word length.

The letter should be short. Two pages is the limit; one page, ideal. But ultimately the letter must be just long enough to do the job for which it has been created—to sell the editor on your article.

With the above in mind, here's a query letter to the editor of *Farmland Times*:

> Dear Mr. Whitsell:
> Horsepower may save the family farm!
> At least that's what Dan Benedict of Sterling, New York, thinks, only the horsepower he is using burns oats instead of gasoline and reproduces its kind. That's right. Belgian work horses—in Dan's case, four Belgian mares.
>
> Dan Benedict is a man not afraid to stand alone, if that is what it takes to get a job done, or to save something in which

he believes. What Dan Benedict believes in is the family farm, and he wants to save it—at least for his four sons.

But Dan Benedict has practical reasons as well for this return to horsepower. He has been able to purchase more productive milkers and thus increase the productivity of his dairy herd while cutting his expenses by a third. Though it takes longer to plow with horses, he finds this is offset by the fact that he can get out onto his wet fields much sooner for spring plowing, and stay on them later in the fall.

Dan Benedict is an unusual man, and what he is doing here is obviously not the answer for every farmer in America. The thrust of this article then will be to portray an American type: the individual strong enough to go his own way.

I suggest a word length of three to four thousand words. There will be interviews with the Benedict family as well as with neighboring farmers. I plan to include pictures of Dan working his team and of the youngest son riding on Daisy, the largest Belgian mare I have ever seen. There will, of course, be a close look at the economics of Dan's operation, along with an honest appraisal of the pros and cons of using work horses today. If you would like to see this article—on speculation, of course—I could have it ready for you within two weeks of receiving your reply.

Sincerely,

Notice that this entire letter is an appeal to the editor's stated preference for articles with a strong human interest that promote farm life. Furthermore, it contains indications of how the writer plans to approach this topic and gives specific indication of just what aspects of the farm operation will be studied closely.

Since this is an example of the kind of query letter a beginning writer might send, notice that it does not contain any mention of the writer's previous credits *or present inexperience*. Never mention in your first queries that you are studying writing and would appreciate any help the editor could give. Let the clarity and interest of the letter speak for your skill, and let that be the sole focus of your appeal.

Notice also that this query letter assured the editor that if he or she didn't like the article, there was no obligation to buy it. That is what the bit about speculation meant. The letter query is a business letter. A very good idea would be for the writer to get hold of a good grammar text, one that contains a clear presentation of the style and format of business correspondence. It goes without saying, I am sure, that this letter—in addition to following the proper business form—should be immaculate, typed without errors, and exhibit a perfect grasp of style, grammar, and punctuation.

After Sending the Query

Some beginning writers become paralyzed after they mail their query letter. They camp by the mailbox and wait for the go-ahead. Nothing could be more foolish—or wasteful.

As soon as that query is on its way, you should look around for more articles and start composing other queries. This means that you will soon have a flock of them in the mail. Of course, you are going to get some negative replies to your queries. No one bats a thousand. But when you do get a no, you can send that query out to other, similar magazines, always being sure to keep a record of where you have sent it.

In summary, the query letter is necessary because it is foolish for you to go to the trouble of preparing an article for a magazine or newspaper that has no interest in looking at your work or has probably published a similar piece recently. Only by writing for those editors who at least agree on the interest value and appropriateness of a particular article for their publication can you hope to compete economically.

To first write an article and then start looking around for an editor or magazine that might be interested in it is a hopelessly scattershot method, similar to shooting blindly into a forest in hopes of bringing down a bear. Of course, a writer may sell a few articles this way. But it is luck, not planning that has brought this about.

The query letter is simply a letter that asks an editor if he or she would like to look over an article you are considering writing—without any obligation to purchase it. Its purpose is to give the writer of an intelligently conceived and executed query letter a go-ahead to write an article the editor might want to publish.

Putting This Chapter to Work for You

1. Earlier you found a topic. Now think of that topic as an arrow looking for a target. Follow your interest and select a magazine you think would be happy to publish your article, do the preliminary research, and compose your query letter.
2. Mail it and promptly go to work on another topic, preliminary investigation, and query letter.

3. Keep track of each query and always retain a carbon copy of each one, noting the letter's destination, day sent, and so on. If the query comes back with a negative scribbled on it, revise it and send it to another magazine.
4. The telephone can sometimes be used in place of a query letter. If you think you have a good idea for a news feature, call up the editor and discuss it with him — being sure to have done enough preliminary legwork on the story to be able to tell the editor quite clearly what you have in mind.

Meanwhile, keep those queries moving.

chapter eleven

My Aunt Was Married to a Gorilla

In fiction it is called the narrative hook. In non-fiction it is the lead. But in either case it is the reason the reader feels he or she has to read what you have written. Without this hook, the reader will move on and you will have lost him or her forever. So let's examine a few leads and see how it's done.

Think of the distractions that tug at us relentlessly. The ballgames we want to watch. The rooms we have to paint. The phones we have to answer. The weekends we have to spend. The promises we have to keep.

We're all caught up and swept along in the same turbulent whirl. When do we find time to read? When we are forced to, when we find ourselves unable not to finish an article or book we have picked up. Good writing—and that presupposes an exciting, snaring opening—is easier to read than not to read. You are pulled in by the force and excitement, the promise, of those few opening lines and find that you have swallowed the hook and must now follow the lines all the way to the end.

To suggest that the writer should not need to rely on this opening device is to ask the reader to give his complete attention to what the writer has written, simply and solely out of the kindness of his heart. That is nonsense. Once out of the classroom few, if any, read what does not demand their attention and hold their interest—from start to finish.

This excitement, this high interest quotient, is what all readers demand. Your reader will be no exception.

The Direct Address Hook

This is in some cases a quite effective way to grab the attention of your reader.

> Maybe it has already happened to you. Arriving back at the garage early, you note your car still parked where you left it, but a bill all ready for you. Or perhaps you paid for an oil change and new oil filter and discover all you got was the new filter. If so, what you have been suspecting is correct: an alarming number of grease monkeys are just fussing around with their greasy cloths when they should be working on your car.

Here is another example:

> The first thing to remember when talking to Groucho Marx is that he is not always cracking jokes. You might laugh, all right. There's not really much you can do about that. But you'll find Groucho's remarks not only side-splitting, but filled with quirky wisdom as well.
>
> It is this aspect of Groucho's personality that fascinated me when I first met him twelve years ago in New York when the two of us . . .

There is nothing wrong with this opener if you don't overdo it, and it is an excellent hook for articles dealing with personal experiences or revelations. Once this method is used to pull the reader in, however, it should be used sparingly thereafter. One real danger is that it might cause the writer to get too familiar with the reader, scolding or patronizing, or ascribing to the reader motives and predilections the writer has no right to assume about anyone but him- or herself.

Hooking the Reader With a Question

Though the question hook is no longer as popular as it once was, it should not be ruled out entirely. It is often used with direct address. Here's how it might be combined with the first of those direct-address openings illustrated above:

> Have you been taken yet? If not, watch out. You may be the next person to arrive back at the garage to find your car parked where you left it, but a bill all ready for you. . . .

What makes this opening effective is that a question is almost impossible to ignore. In spite of all he can do, the reader will find himself formulating an answer—and in the process reading on. But like the direct-address hook, this opener must be handled with a certain amount of discretion, since the very effectiveness of the approach demands respect for the sensibilities of the reader. You have him by the throat. So go easy on him, but not so easy as to lose him.

Here's a question hook that uses an indirect question:

> Perhaps you have wondered of late whatever became of good manners. Could old-fashioned courtesy have disappeared forever? This same question occurred to me not too long ago while joining a heedless swarm of commuters pouring onto the Sixth Avenue subway during the rush hour. I almost lost . . .

This opening doesn't grab the reader as forcefully as the direct-address question, but it gets the job done and seems to fit better the subject of the article. It asks a question and pulls you into the discussion, but it does not hector you in—and this, after all, is an article on courtesy.

Another pitfall of the question hook is that sometimes the writer gets carried away, and instead of one or two judiciously conceived questions, we get a series—a kind of inquisition—that swiftly palls.

Here's what I mean:

> When will the Vietnam War end? Does the president know? Does he care? And what about the wives of the POW's? Certainly they care. But how can they plan as this interminable conflict grinds on? Imagine the frustration of our lawmakers as they try to establish a budget that does not include enormous war expenditures! When will the American people demand an answer to these questions? When will . . .

And when—the reader asks—will this writer get on to the business of the article? Of course, this example is an exaggeration—and in its way probably did much to help end that war—but it is the sort of thing the writer must watch out for with this opening. Note that its best application is in combination with the direct-address hook.

The Startling Fact as Hook

The startling fact as hook is one opener that can be really effective *if and only if* the startling fact is indeed startling. Here's how it works:

> Three out of ten Americans are illiterate. Of course, Madison Avenue has known this for years, and the level of their commercials leads to the conclusion that they consider the number of illiterates to be considerably higher. Be that as it may, this shocking fact is one that our government should—but doesn't—take into consideration when it promulgates its various traffic laws.
>
> Three months ago on highway 104 just outside Pittsburgh, a tractor trailer was just pulling up to one of those multilaned intersections when . . .

In the next example, the humorous nature of the article allows for a little "stretching." But the basic fact is indeed startling:

> My aunt was married to a 475 lb. male gorilla. At least that was what the gorilla seemed to think after living since an infant in our household. My aunt, a sweet little old lady who disdains tennis shoes, and is called Emma by her friends, first discovered Elmer's problem—Elmer is what she called the gorilla—last spring.

She had gone outside to work in the garden when the cleaner drove up, saw her at the back of the house, and started to walk toward her. At that moment . . .

In a less sensational story, your hook might go something like this:

Stalking through the halls of corporate officialdom is the scourge of heart disease. It ends more careers than does cancer, tuberculosis, pneumonia, or any other malady. Yet it can be stopped in its tracks and shackled if the patient does his part. Tidewater Petrochemicals, a division of *Afro Products*, has taken the first step in saving its higher echelon people from this . . .

This hook is a favorite of most writers of feature articles. But unless it is handled correctly, it may get too shrill. Worse, the striking opening statement may have only a tenuous relationship to the substance and theme of the article. The lesson is obvious. Unless you are certain you have a really startling point to make, don't twist your material into a "Believe It Or Not" simply in order to catch the eye of the reader.

Nevertheless, this is still one of the most serviceable openings. Use it when the facts warrant its use.

The Narrative Hook

The narrative hook is becoming exceedingly popular today; the beginning writer should study it carefully. It is an extremely difficult opening to handle smoothly, however, since it requires—as the name implies—an ability to write fictionally.

It is best suited for articles that describe personal experiences and adventure and narrative articles. With these openings the writer uses incidents, conversation, and anecdotes, capitalizing on their inherent dramatic qualities. Here is an example:

The phone rang. Janice Hanlon picked it up and heard the voice of a young girl sobbing hysterically: "Help me!" the voice cried. "Oh, please help me!" And then the sobs drowned out any more words.

Patiently Janice counseled the girl: "Just tell me your name, dear. Just tell me your name and how I can help you. It's all right. You're going to be all right."

Brokenly, the voice on the other end of the line revealed her name and address and the nature of her difficulty. She had deliberately swallowed half a bottle of sleeping pills. Close to passing out entirely, the girl had developed second thoughts and now wanted help.

She got it. Instructing the girl to hang up and start walking around her room, Janice called a fellow volunteer in her unique clinic, who immediately drove to the girl's apartment to give her help. And while help was on the way, a call to the emergency dispatcher at the medical center alerted the authorities.

In this particular case, the girl had a rough three hours in the emergency ward, but she recovered and — as usually happens — became another volunteer in Janice Hanlon's clinic, one more person out there on the other end of the line doing what can be done to see that you or someone you love does not take that final step into oblivion.

Janice Hanlon's Suicide Clinic is what it is called and it has stirred up quite a controversy in this western city. . . .

That opening used an actual case; but sometimes the lead may consist of a fictional though *typical* incident:

There is a faint rustling at the edge of the clearing, and then the buck strides proudly into view, his nose quivering as he explores the wind, magnificent antlers poised atop his alert head.

Time stands still. The whole world appears to be waiting as you lift your rifle slowly and find that ample chest with your sights. Your finger tightens on the trigger . . . and then it happens!

Your hands begin to tremble violently. Sweat stands out on your forehead. Desperately you try to force control on your shuddering arms, but even as you tremble more violently, the buck turns swiftly and bounds off into the brush — and that chance you've been waiting so long for is gone.

Perhaps this dismaying experience has never happened to you, but buck fever rages pretty generally throughout the hunting fraternity. Surprisingly enough, as psychologist Michael Hearne has only recently pointed out, buck fever does not only afflict the greenhorn or the nervous nellies. Experienced hunters may in fact . . .

The so-called descriptive lead is a variant of the above and again uses what are generally regarded as fictional elements. It attempts to lure the reader through the vividness and force of the description, which is usually a static portrait of a man or force of nature:

> Tall, shambling, a great bear of a man is the way one would invariably describe him. But even more noticeable than his great size would be the ruddy face, the thatch of red hair, and the blazing blue eyes that regard one as keenly and as shrewdly as an eagle come warily to rest. Thus does Jimmy Sanford, the most skillful fire fighter on the west coast, first strike one. They call him Red, naturally, and his huge frame is pocked and coiled with the scars of innumerable fires—each one of which he has succeeded in putting out.
>
> There was one fire, however, that Jimmy Sanford could not put out. This was the fire that . . .

Here is another example:

> Unable to clear his mind of the doubts that nagged at him like insistent mice in a wall, Bryant took a walk back along the road his coach had come that day. While he walked, the fading day took on a splendor that caught at his heart. He paused as the glory of that sunset lit the world, and looked skyward. He was just in time to see a lone waterfowl, rushing with swift, powerful strokes of its wings toward the setting sun—and whatever destiny awaited it.
>
> The sight of that lone, intrepid bird on its solitary journey was all the answer Bryant needed. He returned at once to the inn and began the composition of "To a Waterfowl".
>
> Yet the genesis of a poem—like that of a man's life—goes back much farther than these somewhat obvious . . .

The difficulty with the descriptive variant of the narrative opening is that there is always the tendency to overwrite. And this is a danger that must be guarded against vigilantly. However, in a discussion of poets and poetry, a certain willingness to take flight may be what is required; all of which means that your opening hook must be selected on the basis of its suitability for the subject and the magazine for which it is being written.

The Summary Hook

There are times when the best possible way to open your article is with a simple, straightforward summary of what you have to offer the reader. Such an opening intrigues the reader simply because it gives him or her a pretty fair idea of what is to come, and if it seems interesting enough, he or she will decide to read it. This approach has much to recommend it, since it is so honest. It does not try to gimmick the opening or twist the material unduly in order to snag the reader's attention. Nevertheless, it does have to contain enough of interest to excite curiosity, at least:

> Fifteen hundred miles over the Kalahari by Jeep, the looting of heretofore undiscovered tombs, diamonds as large as your fist, shimmering lakes and palm groves, wind-carved hills and sapphire brooks—all within one day of your New York travel bureau. This, with gazelle hunting in the desert and a safari through Hemingway country, is in brief the story of my recent mid-winter holiday. . . .

Another example:

> Before we set out, we knew that the Bahari tribesmen of Borneo were the most savage hunters in the world. What we learned, in fact, was that they are that and more. They are trophy hunters, but elephant isn't their game; there are no elephants left in their corner of the world—and no other large animals of sporting worth to challenge their prowess as killers. The Bahari's quarry is man. They kill and castrate, not always in that order. These are the people we lived among for four years—during which time my wife and I came to understand and love them.
>
> Our first contact with the Bahari came on a bright morning in . . .

The summary hook is not to be despised simply because it is so straightforward. Often a lead constructed on this principle can be just as hard-hitting as any of the more extreme examples of the hook. In some magazines this routine form will present a refreshing simplicity in contrast to the other, more frantic examples of the hook; it may actually be preferred.

Length of the Hook

The hook should be as short as possible, but still carry out its function of attracting attention, introducing the subject, and persuading the reader to read on. This means there cannot be any arbitrary length, but that after it has done those three things it should lead at once into the body of the article.

What you may find after a few abortive attempts is that you

prefer not to write your lead until after you have finished writing the article. Only then will you know what tone you want to create with your lead. This means that as you write the first draft of your article, you will constantly be on the alert for any material or slant you can use in your opening hook.

Titles

Anything that helps to catch the eye of the potential reader can be legitimately regarded as part and parcel of the hook. A good title is as important as that opening sentence and paragraph. Unfortunately, though you may labor long and hard over your title, when you see the article in print, you'll very likely see that the editor has changed or altered the title.

Sometimes you will think it a better title, sometimes you will be disappointed at the change. But there's no help for it by then. Not all editors do this, of course. But most find excellent reasons for doing so, and you'll do well not to complain every time this happens.

Does this mean you should not pay attention to titles? No. You've still got to catch the eye of your first reader, the editor. And a good title is quite important, at least at this point in the life of your article.

In selecting your titles you will find that, like your opening hook, it may not occur to you until after you have finished writing the article. Like the lead, it should be as short as possible, give a good, dramatic capsule of the subject of your article, attract attention, and give the reader a desire to read more. It would not hurt to study the titles in the magazine for which you are writing the article for good working examples of the kinds of titles the editor prefers.

In summary, the opening of your article is very, very important, since it is this that must persuade not only the reader but the editor to take the time to read further. An inept opening reveals to the editor, as does nothing else, the level of professionalism you have reached. This is a fast-moving, frenetic world and unless you can snare your reader's attention quickly, you will not have a reader. This, the editor knows only too well.

Finally, each of these hooks can be and usually are combined by writers as they construct the various openings for their articles. Undoubtedly, you realized this as you studied the examples quoted. There is no reason, for instance, why you cannot combine the startling fact with the direct-address, or the question with the narrative or fictional opening. It should not be difficult to regard the summary as an expanded startling-fact hook. But it matters not if or how you combine them—as long as they pull that reader into your article.

Putting This Chapter to Work for You

1. Look through the magazines comprising the market you are considering and find examples of each of the hooks described in this chapter. Analyze them in terms of whether or not each of them is appropriate for the specific article it leads into. Which hook predominated? Was there any you could not find at all? What were some of the combinations?
2. Construct examples of each one of the hooks listed, using those news items as idea sources. Bring them to class and read them aloud for criticism.
3. By this time you should have written quite a few query letters. To the best of your ability at this stage, write hypothetical leads for each of the projected articles for which you have already written queries. It is understood that you would probably not use the particular hook you prepared in this fashion when it comes time to actually write the article for a waiting editor. Still, it may very well prove excellent practice for the lead you eventually do write.
4. When you get a go-ahead on one of your queries, write a hook for the article—and bring it into class to read aloud for criticism from fellow students and your instructor.

If it holds up, you're on your way—and ready for the next chapter.

chapter twelve
Putting It All Together

At last you've arrived. You thought you'd never get here, didn't you! Your research is finished. You've received an affirmative response to one of your query letters, and you've just gone over some lead possibilities. Now all that remains is for you to sort out the notes, the photocopies of pages, the transcribed interviews, the flyers and brochures and organize them into a coherent whole from which you can write your article.

So let's get going.

Clear your desk. Reduce the bulk of your notes, remove from your desk the periodicals and books you have gathered but no longer need. Move them to a closet or another room where they can be retrieved if you find you need them again. All of the pertinent material from the photocopied pages should be scissored out and the rest tossed aside. Any duplication of material should be filed in the circular file. Notes left after being cut down to size should be sorted into piles according to their eventual placement in the article. Transcriptions of the interviews should also be sorted and cut into segments according to where those portions will appear in the finished article.

The Outline: Order Out of Chaos

Using your query letter as a very rough guide, begin to sort the material into a rough chronology, as follows: the lead, the background, the present situation (where we stand now), the significance of it all, and finally the close.

The listing of topics, if you look at it closely, pretty generally reflects the pattern of most articles; out of this will emerge your working outline. Here are two examples showing how this topic outline may indeed fit altogether dissimilar articles.

The first is a personality piece on a local head football coach winding up 25 years in the same school district. The *lead* would show him in the act of coaching, in particular telling a young halfback around whose shoulders he has draped an affectionate arm that fumbling a football is not the end of the world. A moment later the player, back in the game, breaks a tackle and bursts through the line for a sizable gain. This dramatic opening illustrates the coach's handling of and care of the players under his charge.

Next we shift into *background* and describe the coach physically, give his full name, mention his educational background, note how long he's been at this school, and detail his records both as a player at the state university and as a coach. This is the place in the article where portions of the interview with the coach could be inserted. Naturally, those quotations selected would verify and amplify the picture of the coach being presented in the article.

The *present situation* would bring the reader up to date by mentioning that although the coach is retiring, his football team is once again in contention and a delegation of alumni have asked him to stay on for just one more year, a request he has refused. Again this would be an excellent place to bring in specific comments made by the coach during the interview as to why he feels he should finally retire.

The *significance* of the article would depend on what qualities the coach displayed in the interview and were made evident during his years as a coach. Interviews with some of his players and various townspeople who once played for him would help here, along with statements by the coach himself as to the significance of those 23 years. Perhaps a comment of his would help to sum it up as well as give a lead on the title, something like: "Nice Coaches Don't Always Finish Last."

The *close* could either end with some of the coach's words culled from the interview or from others interviewed in the town. And the article could end on the same narrative note with which it began, with the coach back on the football field exhorting his players to win—but still with concern for them as individuals.

Your second article, on the other hand, might be of a different type entirely, a straight news feature on pollution in the neighborhood, a deliberately controversial slant intended throughout. The subject of the article is the pollution caused by the nearby fertilizer plant as it pumps its wastes into the local stream.

A good *lead* for this article might well be a dramatic description of a soiled river as it coils stickily past an empty beach. Perhaps a lone swimmer has braved the ugly tide, but now stands looking at the uninviting water while he hastily towels himself dry.

A shift now into the *background* reveals that this beach, within the memory of the local inhabitants, was usually a crowded and happy place to take one's family during the dog days of summer. Portions of interviews with some of these people could be used here to underline this point, and also what it was that caused the change, namely the fertilizer factory located ten miles upstream.

The *present situation* would contain, for the most part, an in-depth study of the plant and its effluent policies, and, if possible, interviews with those at the plant who are responsible. Their concern or lack of concern would be brought out in these interviews, along with the concerns of the townspeople as well. Any statistics that might give an idea of the sheer amount of effluent produced by the plant, along with figures that would tell just how much it would cost for the plant to change its policy concerning waste disposal would also be needed here. Finally, some estimation of whether the plant is or is not in violation of federal guidelines regarding the pollution of the town's stream should be made at this point.

If the plant were to close as a direct consequence of not being able to afford the costly devices required to contain the effluent, what would the effect of this be on the town's economy? How many townspeople are dependent on the plant for their livelihood?

When all this has been presented, the *significance* can be summed up. It may be that what all this means for the town is precisely what it means for the nation as a whole—that we either continue to pollute or lose economic viability. Or it may be that this town is rapidly mobilizing itself to reverse the process of pollution, that it has decided it would rather have empty stores than a polluted stream. Whatever the conclusion is, the interviews with the townspeople will tell the writer, and this will become the burden of this section of the article.

The *close* of the article might show a local businessman overseeing the installation of a pool in his backyard as he comments that since he can't swim at the beach anymore, he feels this is a good investment. Besides, business is good and getting better, especially since people have heard that the plant is expanding, starting this fall. Yessir, this is a booming town.

Or the article could close with a return to the lonely beach where the writer interviews a family that has just decided that it really shouldn't chance swimming in the water this afternoon, and that it certainly wished the government would do something. This is the fifth beach they've traveled to this summer and found themselves unable to use. And this beach used to be lovely. They've heard about a citizens' group forming in the area and they are now seriously considering joining it.

In both cases, of course, the narrative or fictional openings were preferred and there was a heavy reliance on interviews with local townspeople as well as on the administrators of the plant. This is because, as mentioned earlier, the best articles are those that reduce the complexities of larger issues to human terms and present them as dramatically as possible.

At any rate, for all practical purposes, this format or outline— *Lead, Background, Present Situation, Significance, Close*—will work in a great many cases. It deserves a try at least with your first article.

Now we are back at the cluttered desk, about to assemble your rough outline. First of all, that source material you feel would fit most naturally into the *lead* portion of your article has already been separated from the rest. Good.

Now glue (I prefer airplane cement) to 8½ by 11" sheets of paper all the snippets of notes, the photocopied pages, the material from brochures, and the portions of the various interviews that you feel are suitable for the lead. This material may cover only one sheet of paper or it may fill several. On the top of each sheet place—in large black letters—the single word, *Lead*.

Do the same now with the rest of your research material, labelling each sheet of paper with the appropriate heading. When you finish, the pages headed *Background, Present Situation,* and *Significance* should be greater in number than either the *Lead* or the *Close,* with perhaps the *Present Situation* containing the most pages. As can be imagined, this would be an excellent way in which to check the balance of the article. If the above ratio of material is not realized, it should alert the writer that something may be wrong.

You now have a somewhat neat stack of pages upon which are glued a wild, but readable, pattern of notes, transcriptions from interviews, photocopied pages—and in some cases references to books (the page and paragraph neatly noted) that you are keeping handy. The first pages are labeled clearly *Lead,* the next *Background;* after that come pages labeled *Present Situation* and *Significance,* with the last few pages marked *Close.* This—in very rough but quite workable form—is your outline. Without further ado, read quickly through this material without pausing to correct or put in any connectives. Just keep reading.

Writing the First Draft

As soon as you have finished this quick but thorough read through of all your notes and material, turn to your typewriter and begin to write. You will find yourself remembering specific material you read and you'll snatch it up, read it over, fit it into your article *and keep on typing.* Soon you'll be going along at a steady clip, writing up a storm as you pull into the article not only the material you have beside you, but also the peripheral impressions you did not realize you had absorbed. Research from other fields may find its way into the article at appropriate junctures. And you keep going until you have finished this—your first—draft.

What has been presented here is, admittedly, only one way among many to get that first draft down on paper. Each writer must and will find his own method. But for now you can use this method. It will get the job done.

The Need for Revision

One of the most difficult things for the beginning writer to accept, it seems, is the need for revision. It is this reluctance on the part of so many to revise that keeps the ranks of professional writers reasonably uncrowded.

Why is there this reluctance on the part of so many students of writing to revise their own work? I do not know, unless it is the mistaken notion that spontaneity and naturalness can only be achieved by writing spontaneously and naturally—that is, without revising—put it down fresh and then don't dare touch it.

As a result of this nonsense, it seems, young writers shrink from the task of rewriting. To them that first draft is something utterly remarkable, immutable even, a creation that must not be altered in any way.

Nothing could be further from the truth. Your first draft is invariably bad and you will simply have to get used to that fact. Once you do, you will find that rewriting can be very exciting. It is a most satisfying experience to see your article grow under your red pencil, to see the excesses pruned, the unnecessary facts deleted, the sweet but useless adjectives swept ruthlessly away, the too digressive paragraphs swiftly excised—in short, to bring order out of the botch that is your first draft.

Writers attack the problem of revision differently. When one quite successful writer finds himself in difficulty, he resorts to pen and paper, writing his sentences over and over again—sometimes as many as twelve, fifteen or eighteen times—until he begins to see his way clear to what he means to say. Only then does he go to his typewriter. But he is still not finished revising as he types and retypes until finally he is sure he has achieved the final crystallization of his idea. When he has finished a page in this fashion, he regards it as complete, pretty much as it will appear later on the printed page. So, page by agonizing page, this writer proceeds. Not every page follows this pattern. Some come easier than others. The lesson is clear: however it is done, every writer must find his or her own way to revise. The question is not should you, but how do you?

How to Rewrite

Read your first draft through quickly. You will probably notice at once that something is wrong—a slight nagging uneasiness that you can't locate specifically. The article seems out of whack perhaps. There is too much documentation of a minor point, while at the same time you do not have enough support for an assertion you lean pretty heavily on later in the article. Your lead seems to go on a little too long and your close is a little draggy.

Yes, these are the large faults, faults in the construction. All right. Many of these items you can fix with the judicious use of the red pencil. Where there seems to be a need for further documentation, you know where to get it and it will be a relatively simple matter to provide it.

With that first stage of the revision out of the way, you can tend to the more subtle weaknesses of your article. You can start clarifying. This means, of course, that you must keep your theme in mind—know precisely what it is you are saying in this article—

and revise accordingly. Whenever your phrasing is muddy, indefinite, recast it. There is absolutely no reason why everything you say should not be clear. Your job as a writer is to clarify, so keep it simple.

Go back to that chapter on style. Is your writing flat, uninspired, about to put you to sleep? Then vary your sentences for emphasis as well as for variety in sentence structure. Are you cluttering your sentences with needless phrases? Are you taking the long way around to say something? If circumlocution is your trouble, get out that red pencil and begin slashing.

Are some of your passages a mite unintelligible? Do you have to explain them to yourself? Read them aloud to see if they say precisely what you mean. Are you aware that your meaning may not be absolutely clear? Then make it clearer!

Do not make the mistake of so many young writers who tell themselves they are not writing for simple clods, that a little complexity lends class to what they write. It doesn't at all. They may not be writing for simpletons, but they *are* writing for people who have more things to do than read the inept prose of any young snob more interested in impressing himself than he is in informing others.

A Checklist

Clean out the adjective pairs, the repetitions. Look for favorite words, phrases, mannerisms, purple patches. Check your connectives to see that you are not overworking the same ones. Are you in the habit of saying *thus* or *therefore* over and over? Dig out a grammar text and look up the list of connectives. Do you use *and*, *then*, *but* too much?

Finally, go over the grammar, the punctuation, the sentences that aren't sentences and should be. Watch out for the comma splice or fault. If you don't know what these terms mean, get a handbook of grammar and make it your business to find out. Go over the spelling. Any word you wouldn't be willing to bet your life on as being correctly spelled is probably incorrect. Look it up.

Keep in mind that as long as you are communicating to your reader clearly and simply so that he understands precisely what you are telling him, your style is in fine working order.

Fitting in the Corrections

Try to do all your corrections on the pages you have typed. Write in whatever additions you have in the margins with arrows from the text indicating where they go. At first glance it will look close to impossible to follow, but the story line of your article will prevent you from getting lost. If you need still more room for corrections, use the other side of the paper. Occasionally you will add a new bit of material or a completely rewritten passage in longhand on a new sheet of paper and fit it in with the others.

But throughout the entire process, as you correct you keep going. It is imperative that you not allow yourself to get bogged down for too long on one page or passage. At last, when you have finished, you should have typed pages covered with corrections—sometimes on both sides—intermingled with freshly written, typed or handwritten pages.

The Final Draft

Now you are ready to start typing up the final copy of your article. As you type, you will find yourself stopping at a word to consider if this is really the one you want. You will begin to make corrections of your corrections.

Sometimes you will push the typewriter away, grab a sheet of blank paper, and proceed to write a portion of the article from scratch (usually these are the difficult, tricky transitional sections of the article, where you are going from one major subdivision to another). You will polish it carefully, take a deep breath, and then type it up as part of the final draft.

And so it will go as this final draft becomes, in some cases, a third draft. It will all be done with incredible care and attention to detail because you will know that this is the copy that goes out to the editor. When you have finished, you should find that some portions of the article are fresh off the top of your head, while others have been gone over time and again. Yet, when you read it over for typing errors, you will find that it all hangs together.

What is the advantage of this method? Surprisingly, it is the fact that this way of revising prevents you from doing too *much* revision, the kind that begins to break down until it becomes a masochistic exercise in self-destruction as you go over and over what you have written until in the end you are not absolutely sure of spelling *cat* correctly. With the method outlined above, you type only two copies of your article: your first draft and your final draft, and during the process of revision, you are urged to keep moving *forward*.

Should You Hire a Typist?

The answer is no—certainly not at this stage. If you will note, I am assuming that this final retyping of the manuscript is also a revision, one that takes place in the white heat of concentration. No typist—no matter how skilled or sympathetic—can do this for you. Some of your most crucial revisions, many that may make the difference between success and failure, occur during the typing of this final, send-to-the-editor copy.

The key here is that you know that this is it, the last copy, the last chance. There will be no more revisions after this one. It is all up to you and the time is now. It is this knowledge that accounts for the concentration that makes it work. You are putting yourself through a wringer, but there is no other way.

Putting it all together may seem arbitrarily mechanical. Writing non-fiction should have more to it, you say. Where's the excitement, the sense of exhilaration that comes with the act of creation? Good writing is an amalgam of sweat, technique, and occasionally inspiration—with all of it coming under the general heading of work.

Though this method of transmuting your mass of source material into an article may seem mechanical, it will get the job done for you now. Later you may want to develop your own method.

Putting This Chapter to Work for You

First you found a topic, then you did enough research to write a query, and now you are waiting for a response to that query to tell you whether or not to go ahead with the article. That's the way it should be.

But here's where you are going to break that rule: even though you may not as yet have received an affirmative to your query, proceed to the writing of your article, remembering the following key points made earlier:

1. Pay special attention to your theme as you finish your research. The facts you unearth should indicate the theme—not your preconceptions.
2. The first thing to worry about after you have finished your research is your lead; but remember, you may not be able to devise the correct lead for your article until you have finished your first draft.
3. Follow the method outlined in this chapter—or one your instructor approves—and write the article. When it is ready for submission to an editor, ask your instructor to look it over.
   If your instructor okays it, go on to the next chapter.

chapter thirteen
Getting-and Staying-Published

You really won't have to worry much about publishing unless you begin to regard this profession seriously—that is as a **business**—which means you must pay attention to details. A few of these details follow.

As you ready your manuscript for the mails, one of your major concerns should be its appearance. This is the first thing the editor will notice as he or she pulls it from the manila envelope.

The editor will either be pleased or disgusted, depending on what he or she finds. You would be astonished at the garbage editors find waiting on their desks. Handwritten manuscripts on grease-stained pages. Whole manuscripts typed with red ink— or in script. Ribbons so far gone that only the impression of the keys gives a clue as to what words might have been typed. Lined tablet paper with gushy notes in the margins that tell the editor how much he or she is going to love this part coming up. Arrogant letters that announce to the editor the arrival of a new writer on the scene, followed by undecipherable gibberish, usually of a pseudo-religious character having to do with universal love. A lot of the manuscripts look as if they were the work of practical jokers. But—incredibly—these people are serious.

Well, serious or not, back it goes by return mail after a quick sniff to verify the first impression. That is, it goes back if a stamped, self-addressed envelope is provided, one large enough to contain the returning manuscript, not the expected check. Otherwise, the manuscript starts on its one-way trip to the incinerator.

Can you imagine the pleasure, therefore, when one of these harried editors pulls out a manuscript that is typed on fresh white bond with what appears to be a newly purchased ribbon? The second glance shows a clearly organized cover page, followed by a neat, spotless manuscript with a bare minimum of corrections, and each one of them done carefully and legibly.

The editor leans back and begins to read, the hook pulling him or her into the article. Maybe this is something he or she can use in the February issue. It's getting close to the deadline and two more articles are needed . . .

Some Hints

Have I made my point? I hope so. First of all, make sure your ribbon is black and reasonably new and the type is clean, so that every "e" doesn't look like an "o". Use a good, medium-weight (16 pound) white bond. Do not purchase so-called "typing paper" sold in bargain department and drug stores or "onion skin" erasable paper. This paper is much too flimsy for manuscripts.

Prepare a cover page for every manuscript you submit. In the upper left-hand corner, type—on three lines—your name, street address, and city or town. These three lines should be single spaced. In the upper right hand corner, indicate the magazine for which the article has been prepared and the approximate length of the article. (Don't count every word; find the average number of words for a couple of pages and multiply by the total pages in the manuscript.)

About one-third down the cover sheet, type the title in caps. Underneath this, in a neat paragraph indicate the basic source or sources of material, and then make a list of pictures, if you are including any. (Don't send negatives, just glossy prints.)

On the first page of the manuscript, repeat the information in the upper left and right corners of the cover sheet. One third down the sheet repeat the title and subtitle, as on the cover sheet.

The texts of all manuscripts are typed double-spaced. There are no exceptions to this rule. Number every page in the upper right-hand corner and put your name in the upper left. The margins must be ample enough to allow for editorial corrections and notation. Leave at least 1½ inches on all four sides.

Some Typing Hints

If you are not a professional typist, here are some instructions that might help:
- To indicate italics underline just the word.
- A dash is two hyphens between the words, with no space before or after each hyphen. Do *not* use a single hyphen with a space on either side to indicate a dash since a hyphen is used to connect words, not separate them. If you let single hyphens serve as dashes, the editor will have to go over each one with a pencil to correct it.
- To indicate transitions between sections stay away from the asterisks and other fancy devices. Simply skip four spaces.
- Quotations longer than four sentences should be indented on both sides, the quotation marks omitted. Otherwise, use quotation marks with the material typed in with the main text. When you are omitting words from quotations, use three periods (ellipses) only to indicate the missing words. To indicate this fact at the end of the sentence, use four periods—no more.
- Leave a single space after a comma, and leave two spaces after a period.

Submitting the Manuscript

As indicated above, the manuscript's appearance will do much toward insuring it the respectful attention of the editor. This should be enough. Any letters you enclose are liable to be exercises in laboring the obvious. You do not need to tell the editor that he or she is looking at a manuscript and that you hope he or she likes it. The editor knows what you hope; he or she has opened manila envelopes containing manuscripts for longer than he or she would care to remember.

However, if you have a really special expertise in the subject matter of your article (you lived for twenty years with the headhunters of the Upper Amazon), or if this manuscript is being sent to the editor as a result of a favorable response to your query letter, a covering letter is acceptable and in the latter case advisable.

In the covering letter state as briefly as possible that this is the article the editor expressed an interest in seeing. Then stop and let your manuscript speak for itself.

Always enclose another manila envelope, folded double usually, with your address on it and stamps to pay for the article's return passage, if such is the will of fate. Send the manuscript flat no matter how small it is, with a cardboard to keep it from getting wrinkled or damaged, and send it first class—unless you're willing to wait a long, long time. The manuscript should be addressed to the editor with whom you corresponded earlier, or if you are sending the article out cold (I do not recommend this), to the editor listed in the market report for that magazine.

Do not staple the pages of your manuscript together. If you must fasten them, use paper clips; but even this precaution is frowned upon by some editors. Under no circumstances enclose the article in one of those transparent plastic holders.

Should Your Article Be Copyrighted Before You Submit It?

Don't worry about publishers stealing what you send to them. Of all the bogeymen that frighten young writers, this is the most common and the most silly. The editor will tell you what rights he is purchasing, if any. Magazines are copyrighted by the issue and the copyright to all materials printed in each issue belongs to the publishing company. If you want reprint or foreign rights later, simply write to the magazine and ask that the copyright for your article be assigned to you.

Meanwhile, don't worry. When you get big enough to worry about copyrights, you'll be wise enough to know all about them.

Keeping a Record

There should be a carbon copy of every query and manuscript you type. This carbon is insurance against loss. (Yes, editors as well as the post office have been known to lose manuscripts.) This precaution also provides you with a draft of your article on hand if the editor wants you to make a few changes. Last but not least, it retains for your files a considerable fund of information that you worked pretty hard to gather. You may very well find this research useful in the future for other, related articles.

At first you will find it difficult to imagine that you could forget where you sent your manuscript. But soon there will be other children of yours out there in manila envelopes looking for a home. And after a delay of six weeks or more, you will find yourself just a little uncertain as to where you sent them all—and when.

Some writers purchase a file cabinet. Within each file envelope they place a carbon of their query letter and the carbon of the article that resulted. On the cover page of the article they note where the article was sent and when. Every time it returns and is sent out again, a notation to that effect is made on the cover sheet.

In addition, it is usually a good practice to include an accounting of the expenses incurred while writing the article, not failing to mention postage to the magazine and return postage included. This information should be placed into the same file envelope as the carbon copies of the query letter and the article.

For each new query letter and article, a new file is created.

The Return of the Prodigal

It happens. Instead of a fat check, back comes the fat manila envelope, your own handwriting penning the address, your own stamps on the envelope. What to do? It is, admittedly, not a good omen with which to start the working day.

What the professional writers do is simple. They sit down at their desk, look over the article, select another likely market for it, type a second query letter to the appropriate editor, making it fit in with this other editor's stated requirements or slant, then mail the query and get back to work on the other article they have been working on.

If the writer gets a favorable reply to this second query letter, he or she reworks the article wherever it is necessary to make sure it fits this other magazine's slant, and sends it along. Incidentally, it is always a good idea to wait a decent interval after receiving the go-ahead from the second editor before sending this previously rejected article out to him or her, so that the editor will not think either that the writer is a genius to have written the article so swiftly, or the truth—that this is a rejected article on its second, possibly third round.

For the same reason, the article should arrive on each editorial desk as crisp and clean as if it just popped from the typewriter. The writer retypes, therefore, any page that shows signs of wear—the whole manuscript, if necessary.

Not until the writer has sent his or her article to every possible market does he or she give up on it. Then he or she places it back into the file. The writer knows the facts in it can be used in another article.

Do You Need an Agent?

No. As you have probably noticed by now, the non-fiction writer is working closely with editors to meet their needs. He or she writes them a query letter and they respond. The writer then proceeds to furnish what the editor wants. In the fast moving world of magazine publishing, this is done as quickly and as economically as possible. There is literally not enough time for an agent.

Sometimes an agent can come between an editor and a writer. He or she is a third party who often confuses matters. Some agents have even been known to turn down lucrative assignments for their writers because they did not think the writer was interested in or capable of doing the job—only to find much later that they couldn't have been more wrong on both counts.

Besides, an agent won't take you on unless and until you are already making money at your craft. And by that time, you'll be off on your own. You may eventually get so big that you will need an agent to keep the editors off your neck. When you do get that big, I suggest you decide for yourself if you need an agent or not.

What Do You Do While Waiting to Hear?

As implied by all that has gone before, as soon as you put one query in the mail, you should be busy working on other queries, investigating other article ideas, researching, studying the *Reader's Guide* to see what has or has not been covered recently and what information is available as you size up other writing projects.

In the weeks that must elapse before you hear from an editor about your original query, you will have ample time to work on other projects while you continue to research the article you proposed originally. Then, as each affirmative query comes in, accelerate your research and proceed to write the articles required.

Now you know why the professional writers keep records.

You and the Market

Whatever you might find between the covers of this book concerning specific magazine needs would be hopelessly out-of-date by the time you read it. It is and will continue to be your business to know your market. Apart from prowling constantly through magazine racks in drugstores, bookstores, and libraries, your best source for information concerning this volatile market is the information you get from those two writers' magazines mentioned previously, *The Writer* and *Writer's Digest*, plus the annual hardbound books, *The Writer's Handbook* and *Writer's Market*.

In these magazines and books you will find listings of every conceivable market for articles. The magazines will be especially helpful, since they keep monthly updates on the magazine market, noting address changes, editorial changes, and so on. Consulting the monthly listings these magazines provide is the only possible way for you to keep up until you have established such a rapport with editors that they will make it their business to keep you informed of their needs personally.

Establishing a working knowledge of your market will take up considerable time—especially at the beginning of your writing career. But do not begrudge this time. You cannot meet a need you do not know exists. Knowing your market is a matter of survival for you as a writer. It is that important.

How Much Money Can You Expect?

Not very much at first, even though there are cases on record of young neophytes selling to a big paying market first time out. But usually this is a fluke. Only after years of steady effort and, as a result of this effort, the writer's growing reputation in the field as a consistent professional, can the freelance writer expect to pull in big checks consistently.

So the young writer starts where the demands and the checks are not so large. News feature articles for local weeklies and dailies, larger articles for the Sunday supplements, will give you only about five or ten dollars a shot, sometimes less. But you will see your material in print and begin to master the intricacies of researching and writing, while learning to live with the realities of the deadline.

But this should only be a start for you.

There are other markets out there, and you should find them. As mentioned earlier, a knowledge of the market is essential for any kind of success in the freelance non-fiction field. This is doubly true if any kind of financial success is desired. You must study the market lists not only to find markets for your material, but also to find out what the rates of the magazines you are contemplating writing for are—and whether or not they pay on acceptance or on publication, a very important consideration I will discuss later.

111

In general, the slimmer the magazine's circulation and the more specialized and limited its audience, the less the magazine can afford to pay. One instance of this is the magazine *The New England Guide*, which wants articles up to 800 words on offbeat New England history. This market pays only $40, and that on publication.

The New England Guide is one example of a general magazine, one that sells regionally to families interested in many general topics—a smaller edition of the once common general interest magazines, such as the *Saturday Evening Post*, *Colliers*, and *Liberty*. The *Colorado Quarterly* is also a regional magazine that caters to a special audience and is a member of the college, literary, and little magazine field. The *Colorado Quarterly* pays only $20 for an article, while another member of this group, *Antioch Review*, pays $8 per published page, on publication. This is actually quite high for the little magazine category, since for the most part, they pay their contributors either with copies of the issue or in prestige. This may be enough for a start, but most writers wish more for their effort—and who is to blame them?

The religious and denominational magazines also pay very poorly, but they do pay something, and this market may well be a good starting point for the beginning non-fiction writer. The rates in this field range from the 2/3¢ a word paid by *Contact* to the $1,000 per article paid by *The American Zionist* and *The Christian Herald*.

The sports, outdoor, travel, recreation, and conservation field is a much better paying market—again with a very wide range of rates. Some of the best paying are *Field and Stream*, which pays $300 and more for full length articles, *The National Geographic*, which pays $1,500 to $3,500 and up if you can give them the kind of articles they specialize in publishing, and *Sports Illustrated*, a weekly that goes as high as $750 for lead articles on major sports figures. In general, however, the average payment in this field is closer to that which *Florida Sportsman* pays: $50 to $100 for an average length article.

The home and garden and women's magazines pay considerably better, though even in this field there are some publications that pay nothing at all, such as *California Homeowner*. But *Good Housekeeping* will pay $1,000 for a full length feature article, which again pretty well illustrates the range of rates in this category. Only by consulting the writer's magazines can the freelancer hope to keep abreast.

The trade and business magazines average $75 to $100 per article, depending on length. The *Auto Glass Journal*, for instance, offers 5¢ a word, while *World Oil* pays $17.50 a printed page, which means you wait until the article is published before you get your money and before you know just how much that will be. This field, however, is very large. Most writers who specialize in trade journals become enormously prolific, churning out countless articles a year by keeping in constant touch with the editors of such magazines, thus enabling themselves to fill immediate editorial needs within days.

The men's magazine field is usually cited by those who feel there must be loads of money in writing articles. This is true if you hit the better paying markets consistently. You can receive as much as $3,000 for a lead article in *Playboy*, but you can also get as little as $100 to $300 for a lead article published in *Knight*. The range can be great within magazines themselves: *Argosy* pays $400 to $750 for non-fiction, while *True*'s rates range from $250 to $1,500.

The general interest magazines have just as great a range of payments, from "about $50" on acceptance from *The American Scandinavian Review*, to $250 to $300 "average" for an article accepted for publication in *Yankee*, to $350 to $1,000 for an article accepted by *Esquire*. Top rates would go even higher for *McCalls* or *Mademoiselle*.

What this means is that the average payment in the best markets is between $200 and $400 for an average length article, with considerable variation above that level and below it. As a freelance writer of non-fiction you must keep a large volume of material in the mail, therefore, if you are to earn enough to keep going as a writer. And you *must* know your market, for only by studying it can you know which are the best paying markets and what to expect when you send out a finished product.

Finally, the writer should submit articles to those markets that pay on publication *only after all other possible markets that pay on acceptance have been exhausted*. Generally speaking, markets that pay on publication are of the less solvent variety—and goodness only knows how long an individual editor is going to want to hold onto an article before he or she decides to fit it into the publication schedule. Personally, I would never submit an article to a magazine that pays on publication. But, of course, many writers do.

Now let me say it just once more: study the market!

Specializing

Since the market for non-fiction is so vast and complex, it would be wise for the beginning writer to specialize in a particular area at first. All professional writers find they do much better when they settle on one field. Some specialize on schools and education, others in popularization of medical topics and related scientific developments, another in odd bits of historical nuggets mined for human interest and drama.

In each the writer is following his or her interests, and establishing his or her credentials as an expert in the field. Once this expertise is established, the writer finds that editors aware of his or her work begin requesting articles.

There are other advantages as well.

Specialization saves time and effort. Instead of having to dig out entirely new material from scratch with each article, the writer goes from one related topic to another in his or her chosen field with a minimum of new digging required in each case.

This specialization increases the writer's accuracy and thoroughness. The more knowledgeable the writer becomes in his or her field, the more able he or she is to separate the chaff from the wheat in research and interviews. Surprisingly, as indicated earlier, the more the writer gets to know about a particular field, the more he or she finds to write about.

In summary, it is obvious that writing non-fiction is a business, and the more businesslike you become, the more time you will find you have to write the articles you will need to produce if you are to stay in print. Once filing, productive researching techniques, typing, grammar, a clear and lucid style, and systematic researching of the market become second nature, you will have become a professional.

Putting This Chapter to Work for You

1. This chapter tells it as it is: Non-fiction writing is a business — in order to succeed, you must become an efficient businessman or businesswoman as well as writer. Does this annoy or dismay you? Are you offended by this emphasis on the commercial aspects of a writing career?

    Write a well-reasoned response to those questions — and bring it in to class for discussion. Attitudes are very important in writing, sometimes crucially so, and you should get this business of the business of writing clear before you can hope to progress much further.

2. If you are serious about a writing career, see how many of the suggestions contained in this chapter you can put to use immediately. (A small filing cabinet can be picked up for a fairly

reasonable price; you should be able to pay for it with your first substantial sale.)

At any rate, keep the queries and the articles percolating. By now, hopefully, you have become idea-conscious — aware, for perhaps the first time, of the wealth of writing opportunities that abound on all sides, just waiting to be captured on paper.

3. Meanwhile, keep the article you have already written in readiness for a favorable response from that editor to whom you wrote the query letter — and if the response isn't favorable, do as this chapter suggests: try other magazines and keep busy.

chapter fourteen

Now That You Are a Writer

By this time you should have found out that you are—or are not—a non-fiction writer. If you have completed an article, have sent a query letter on its way, and are now hard at work on the next one, it's a pretty safe bet that you're hooked. What follows then are a few parting words of advice concerning this fascinating—and bedeviling—craft.

You must undoubtedly have discovered this by now, but in case you haven't, I would like to emphasize one very obvious fact: inspiration is perspiration. It will do you absolutely no good at all to wait for the mood to come on you before you consider sitting down to work at the typewriter. Once you have completed your research, the writing begins, and there should be no nonsense about it.

Does this mean that you are never inspired, never write on the wings of enthusiasm? Of course not. It means only that inspiration—so-called—comes more often than not *after* you have started to write, if it is going to arrive at all.

If inspiration does not arrive, the professional writer keeps on writing nevertheless. He or she keeps at a steady pace without looking back, aware that he or she will do fine during some stretches and poorly during others—and that over all, there will be little appreciable difference in the quality of his or her output.

This should be your attitude as well.

Do You Need More Research?

Watch out for this one. Like a swimmer approaching the water, the non-fiction writer is reluctant to jump into the actual writing of his or her article and will often use this imagined need for still more research as a dodge to keep him or her from sitting down in front of that typewriter.

This is natural. Writing is a lonely business. And after all that exciting legwork, the interviews, the bustling about from library to PR offices, this sudden isolation can be a bit forbidding. But there's no help for it. The paradox of the non-fiction writer is that he or she must be a sociable, easy-going extrovert while gathering material, but a solitary monk or nun while putting it all down.

Recognize this fact and face it. Do not allow your dislike for the isolation required to write your article to be masked under the heading of "need for more research."

It is, admittedly, a difficult line to draw, but you must do it. Better to start your article too soon than too late. This is just one more very good reason for the query. Once you have an okay from an editor, you also have a deadline. Under that circumstance, it is very difficult indeed to dawdle.

I said difficult. I did not say impossible.

The Daily Schedule

Once you start putting the article together you should establish a writing schedule, a time and place each day where you will go and write without hindrance and without distractions.

Writing in this fashion will give you the writing habit. You will develop a self-discipline toward writing that will become so ingrained that whenever you fail to complete your day's work at the typewriter, you will actually feel guilty.

Does It Get Any Easier?

Of course it does. But paradoxically, the more you learn about your craft, the more difficult it will become to satisfy you. Others may be pleased, but seldom you. You will always be trying something a bit beyond your grasp as a writer.

You'll read over some of your published articles and see passages that should have been tightened, instances where you could have probed deeper, summations or openings that could have been written cleaner. You'll notice the mannerisms of your style, the sometimes leaden quality of your sentences, and feel only a quiet fury that you let them get away from you. This next article, you promise yourself, will be cleaner, sharper, more on target.

And this is how it goes for the craftsman.

It is my hope that somewhere between the covers of this book you found what you needed to sustain you in your quest to become a freelance writer of non-fiction.

Good luck.

Index

A

Agent, need for 110
American Library Association 55
American Men of Science 56
Archives, National 58
Arthur Fields Books, Inc. 4
Article types 20–29
    how-to-do-it 28–29
    investments 27
    narratives 23–26
    news feature 20–21
        sources 21–22
    personalities 22–23
    profile 22–23
    self-improvement 26–28
Attitudes of writers 74

B

Biographies, use of in research 54, 55
Biography Index 56
Brevity 49–50

C

Card catalogue 55–56
Cassettes, use of in research 37, 62–63
Catalogue cards 55
    author 55
    subject 55
    title 55
Chamber of Commerce, local, use of in
    research 58–59
Checklist for writers 101
Circumlocution 48–50, 52
Compensation 76–77, 111–13
Congress, Library of 56
Copyrighted material, use of 65–66
Copyrighting your material 108
Credibility, qualifications for 27–28
Curiosity, need for in writing
    non-fiction 14–15

D

Dictionaries, for use in research 55, 57
*Dictionary of Information Resources in
    the United States* 58
Dictionary of National Biography 56
Direct address hook 86–87
Discipline of the professional writer 15–16
Draft, final 99, 102

E

Encyclopedias for use in research 54, 55, 57

F

Facts
   need for 8-9
   pursuit of 53
"Fast read" 48
Fiction, non-fiction differences 7-11
Finalization 11, 12, 43-69
Footnotes 34, 216, 217

G

Government Printing Office 57-58
Government, as source of research 57-58
Guide to Reference Books 55
Guides in libraries, for use in research 55

H

Hobbies, importance of to the writer 74-75
Hooks
   direct address 86-87
   narrative 85, 89-91
   question 87-88
   startling fact 88-89
   summary 91-92
   length of 92-93
How-to-do-it articles 28-29

I

Indexes for use in research 22, 55, 57
Intelligibility, lack of in writing 50-51
Interlibrary loan service in libraries 56
Interviews 34, 37-41, 59, 60-66

123

L

Lead 85–93, 97, 98
Librarian, use of 54, 55, 56
Library of Congress 56
Library, special 56–57
Library, use of 54

M

Manuscript
    carbon copies of 108–9
    preparation of for mailing 106
    return of 109–110
    submission of 107–108
    typing of 102–3, 105, 106–7
Market for non-fiction 19–29, 110–11
    selection of 80
    query 79–83
    specializing in 113–14
Mudge, I.G. 55

N

Narrative hook 85, 89–91
Narratives 23–26
National Archives 58
Needs satisfied by non-fiction 9–10
Non-Fiction
    differences between fiction 7–11
    limits 9
    needs satisfied by 9–10

O

Outline of article 96–99

P

Paragraphing 51–52

Pay.. 76–77, 111–13
Periodicals, use of 57
Personality sketches 22–23
Pictures, use of 66–69
Point of view 37–41
Powers, Thetis 4
Profile sketches 22–23
Prospects for non-fiction writer 3–5
Public relations offices, use of in research 57
Publishing details 105–114

Q

Qualifications for validity and credibility 27–28
Query 79–80, 81–83
Question hook 87–88
Quoting from materials 65–66

R

Reader's Digest 25
Reader's Guide to Periodical Literature 55
Recording during interview 62–63
Reference desk in libraries, use of 55
Reference tools 55–56
Research 8–9, 14, 34, 53, 76, 80–81, 118
Revision 33, 50–51, 99–102

S

Selection of target magazine 80
    query 79–83
Self-improvement articles 26–28
Sentence structure 46–48, 51, 52

125

Seriousness, need for in writing non-fiction 15–16
Significance of non-fiction to reader 9–10
Simplicity 48–50
Source materials 80
Special Library Resources 56
Startling fact (as hook) 88–89
Style 29, 43–52, 101
Subjects (*see also* Article types) 76
Summary hooks 91–92

T

Tape recording 37
Theme
    formulation of 33–34
    significance of 32–34
Topics (*see also* Article types) 76
Titles 93–94
Typing of manuscript 102–3, 107

V

Validity, qualifications for 27–28

W

Who's Who in America 56
Writer, The 80, 111
Writer's Digest, The 14, 80, 111
Writer's Handbook, The 111
Writer's Market 111